HOW YOUR BODY WORKS

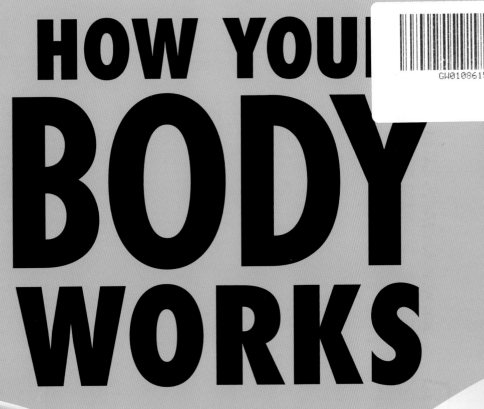

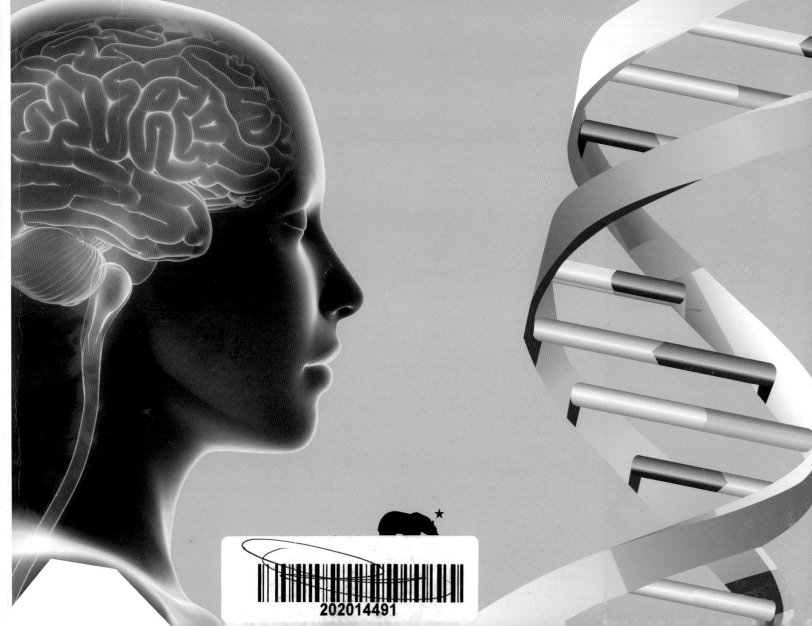

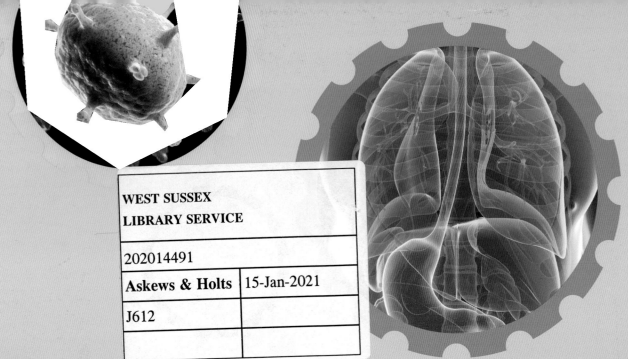

ARCTURUS

This edition published in 2020 by Arcturus Publishing Limited
26/27 Bickels Yard, 151–153 Bermondsey Street,
London SE1 3HA

Copyright © Arcturus Holdings Limited

Author: Thomas Canavan
Editors: Joe Harris, Joe Fullman, Nicola Barber, and Sam Williams
Designer: Elaine Wilkinson
Original design concept: Notion Design
Cover design: Steve Flight

ISBN: 978-1-83940-281-4
CH004189NT
Supplier 29, Date 0420, Print run 10010

Printed in China

Picture Credits:
Key: b-bottom, m-middle, l-left, r-right, t-top
All images courtesy of Shutterstock, apart from:
Corbis: p65 bl; Corbis/Christian Hartmann: p98 b. iStock.com: p29 br.
Science Photo Library: p76 l, p94 tl, p50 m (Michael Abbey),
p81 bl (John Bavosi), p108 ml (Biophoto Associates), p81 br,
p95 tl (Steve Gschmeissner), p38 (Dorling Kindersley),
p97 ml (Jacopin/BSIP), p77 t (Laboratory of Molecular Biology/MRC),
p82 l (Medical RF. com), p91 ml (Omikron).

SCIENCE TECHNOLOGY ENGINEERING MATHEMATICS

What is STEM?

STEM is a world-wide initiative that
aims to cultivate an interest in
Science, Technology, Engineering, and
Mathematics, in an effort to promote
these disciplines to as wide a variety
of students as possible.

CONTENTS

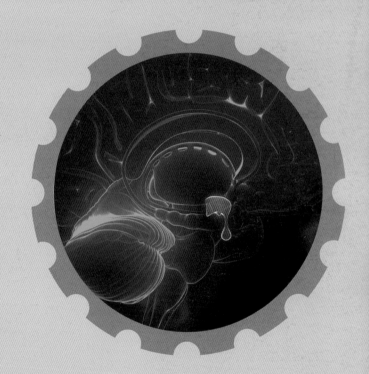

BUILDING

Your body is like a machine that's revving up and raring to go! But it's more amazing than any normal machine. Just think of all the incredible things your body can do: climbing trees, riding a bike, solving puzzles. It's remarkable!

Your body is special because it's totally different from anyone else's body. But at the same time, it's made from the same basic materials as everyone else. Tall or short, white or black – every one of us is a human being, and we're made of exactly the same ingredients. It's just how some of those ingredients are mixed around that makes us different.

ALL IN THE MIX

Everything you see around you is made from a collection of basic materials called chemical elements. Your body is just the same. It's a wonderful mixture of different bits of matter that all add up to make ... you!

IN YOUR ELEMENT

Scientists have identified 118 different basic materials or chemical elements. More than 99 percent of your body is entirely made from just six of these elements. Some of these elements work on their own and have special jobs. Others team up with other elements to build you up and keep your body super healthy.

Oxygen (61%)
This flows through your blood to give you energy.

Carbon (23%)
A building block for every cell in your body.

Hydrogen (10%)
Along with oxygen, hydrogen makes up the water that is found throughout your body.

Nitrogen (2.6%)
Important for growth and digestion.

Calcium (1.4%)
Helps build teeth and bones while looking after muscles.

Phosphorus (1%)
Like calcium, it helps build strong bones and teeth.

Trace elements (1%)

ADDED EXTRAS

The elements that make up the last 1 percent of your body are known as trace elements. A healthy diet allows your body to get all the trace elements it needs from food. For example, salt contains sodium and chlorine. Meat and fish contain iron. Potassium is found in fruits such as bananas. Sometimes, important trace elements are added to particular foods or drinks. Iodine is sometimes added to salt, and many breakfast cereals have added iron.

Salt is important for digestion and helps to balance the fluid in your body.

Iron carries oxygen all around your body and helps it to store and use oxygen.

Potassium helps to regulate how much water your body stores.

ACTIVITY

Take a fortified breakfast cereal and check that it has added ingredients. Crush some cereal in a bowl and add water. Then, use a bar magnet and stir right to the bottom of the bowl. Now, look at the magnet. The black "dust" on it is iron.

The average human body contains enough carbon to make

900

pencils!

BODY BUILDER

At the smallest level, your body is made up of atoms, which are tiny, non-living pieces of elements such as iron or oxygen. Atoms join together with other atoms to form molecules. Molecules are not alive, either. It takes trillions of molecules organized in a very specific way to make the smallest living thing – a cell.

Muscular system

Skeletal system

SYSTEMS GO!

At the largest level, your body is made up of systems. Each system does a particular job. The framework of bones that supports your body is called the skeletal system. The tubes that carry blood from your heart all around your body make up the circulatory system. All the systems work together to keep you going.

Respiratory system

Circulatory system

Digestive system

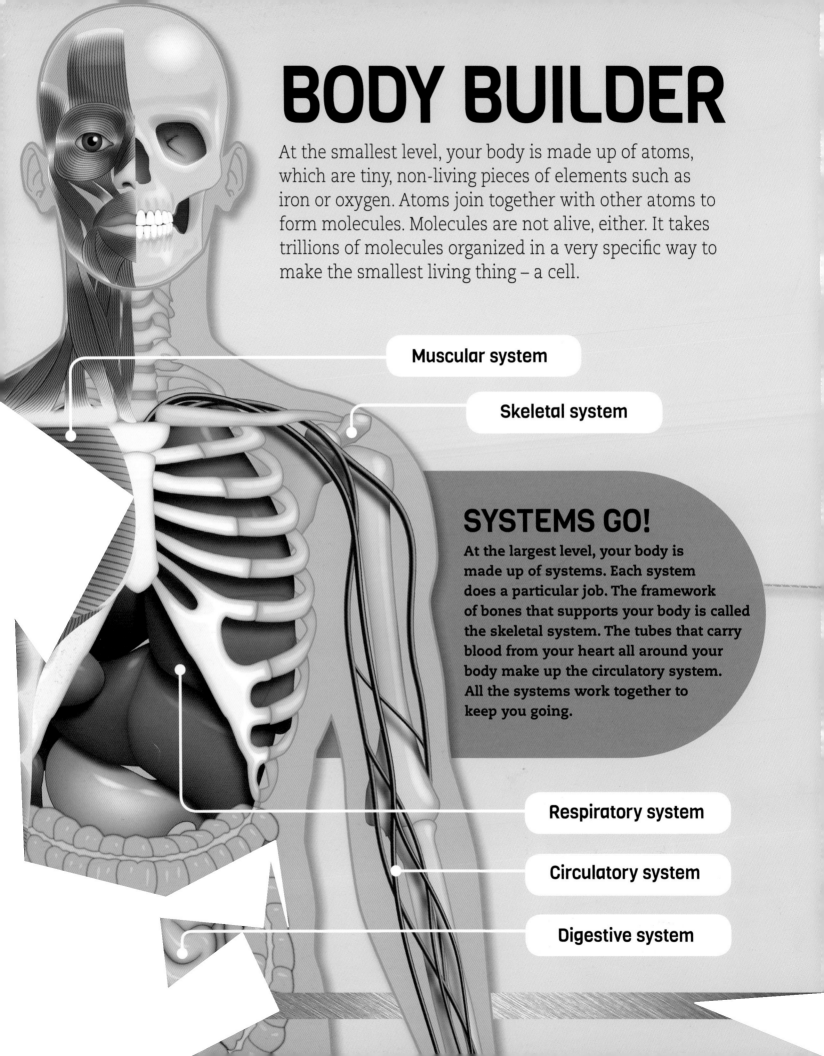

PULLING TOGETHER

There are more than 200 types of cells in your body, and each has a different role. Cells of one type team up to make a tissue. It's the tissue that does the real work in your body! Muscle tissue is made of muscle cells, and is used for pushing and pulling. Other types of tissue do other important jobs.

GETTING ORGANIZED

Two or more types of tissue can combine to make organs. The organs are the major parts of the body, such as your eyes, your kidneys, or your heart. Groups of organs are called systems.

WHAT MAKES YOU?

ATOMS
make up

MOLECULES
which make up

CELLS
which make up

TISSUES
which make up

ORGANS
which make up

SYSTEMS
which make up

YOUR BODY!

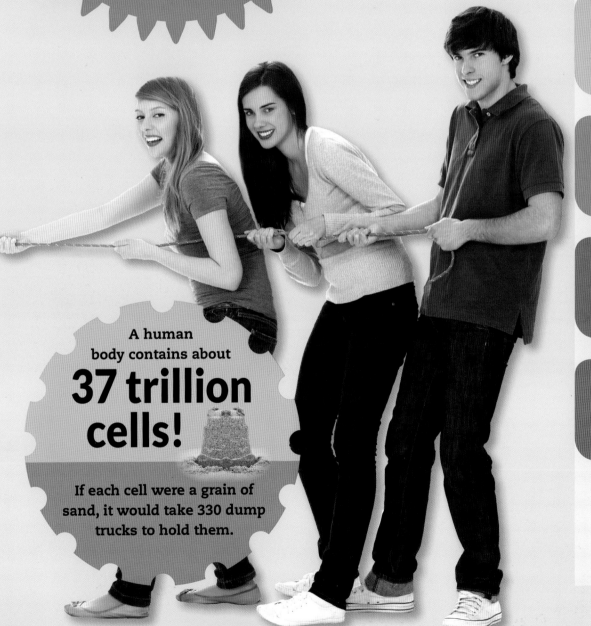

A human body contains about

37 trillion cells!

If each cell were a grain of sand, it would take 330 dump trucks to hold them.

BACK TO BASICS

Your cells are constantly working. They take nutrients (important ingredients) from the food you eat and change those nutrients into energy. They do many different specialized jobs. For example, they fight disease and get rid of waste. They also store instructions about the future – how much you'll grow, whether you'll have curly or straight hair, and what sort of features you'll pass on to your own children. Cells also have to reproduce, which adds even more to their incredible "to do" list!

Cells don't live as long as the person they make up. Some types die after a few days; others live up to a year.

MADE FOR THE TASK

Depending on where they are, and the job they have to do, cells have different shapes.

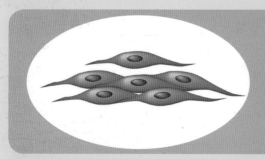

MUSCLE CELLS
These are long and tube-shaped. They can change shape by contracting – squeezing up to make themselves short. When many muscle cells contract at once, they move your body about.

NERVE CELLS
These are long and thin, and have branching end parts that allow them to carry messages to other cells. They connect to each other so that information can be sent quickly around your body.

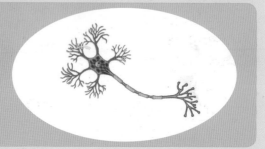

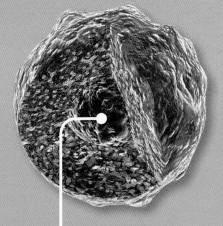

"MINI-ORGANS"

Each of your cells contains special parts called organelles. These carry out jobs to keep the cell active and useful. Some act like tiny factories, making useful molecules for the cell. Others transport molecules from one place to another. Some of the most important molecules are called proteins.

COMMAND HQ

The headquarters of the cell is called the nucleus. The nucleus contains an incredibly important type of protein, called DNA. This is the special code that instructs the cell about what to do and how to develop. So it is the nucleus that directs how the cell will grow – and when it's time to die.

Endoplasmic reticulum: helps the cell make and transport molecules.

Ribosomes: put together the proteins of the cell.

Centrioles: important for cell reproduction.

Nucleus: where the DNA is stored.

Golgi apparatus: sorts, organizes, and sends molecules to the right places in the cell.

Mitochondria: convert food energy into a form that the cell can use.

Plasma membrane: this protects the cell but lets helpful materials through.

Your First Weeks

▲ At 4 weeks
You are a tiny blob no bigger than a poppy seed.

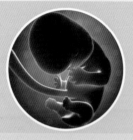

▲ At 8 weeks
Your heart begins to beat. Your body begins to take shape.

▲ At 16 weeks
You're about 10 cm (4 in) long.

At 24 weeks
Hair begins to grow and you sleep and wake regularly.

At 36 weeks
You're running out of room to move and are almost ready to be born.

SMALL BEGINNINGS

Your body might have around 37 trillion cells now, but amazingly, you started out from just one cell! This cell divided into two and, over the course of about nine months, the cells kept dividing and dividing, again and again. As the cells divided, you changed from a tiny blob to a bigger blob and finally to a fully formed, small human being.

IN THE WOMB

All of this growing happened inside your mother's womb, or uterus, for about nine months before you were ready to be born. During that time your organs developed and you began to look more and more human. Being inside meant that you relied on your mother for oxygen and food, which came from an organ called the placenta through the umbilical cord – a tube that went into your stomach.

A mother-to-be can feel the baby inside her kicking from as early as four months into the pregnancy.

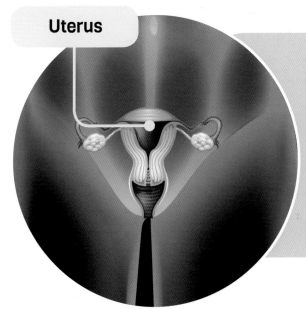

Uterus

BEFORE YOU BEGAN

Every month, an egg cell the size of a small pinhead is released inside your mother's uterus. This egg is ready to be fertilized, which means that it can combine with a sperm cell from your father. However, if no sperm cell is there to combine with it, the egg cell will be washed away.

RACE FOR THE EGG

About nine months before you were born, an incredible race took place – 300 million sperm cells, produced by your father, swam their way through special tubes to reach your mother's single egg cell. Only a few hundred of those made it to the egg. And only one of those cells actually broke through the cell membrane – the protective coating of the egg cell. Together your father's sperm and your mother's egg form a single cell known as the fertilized egg cell.

NINE MONTHS

The fertilized egg cell grew and divided again and again… leading to your nine months developing inside your mother's uterus. We humans are complicated creatures, so we need to develop over a long time before we're ready to be born. But some creatures take even longer – elephants wait two years before they are born!

EGG MEETS SPERM

First, sperm cells enter the uterus.

Only around 200 sperm reach the single egg cell.

One sperm breaks through the cell membrane.

The sperm nucleus merges with the egg nucleus.

BRAND NEW YOU

Imagine spending nine months inside the same room, when that room seems to be getting smaller and smaller as you get bigger and bigger. That's what it's like when you're ready to be born. Things have become uncomfortable for you – and for your mother. You don't need to be inside there anymore, so it's time to see the outside world. It's your birthday!

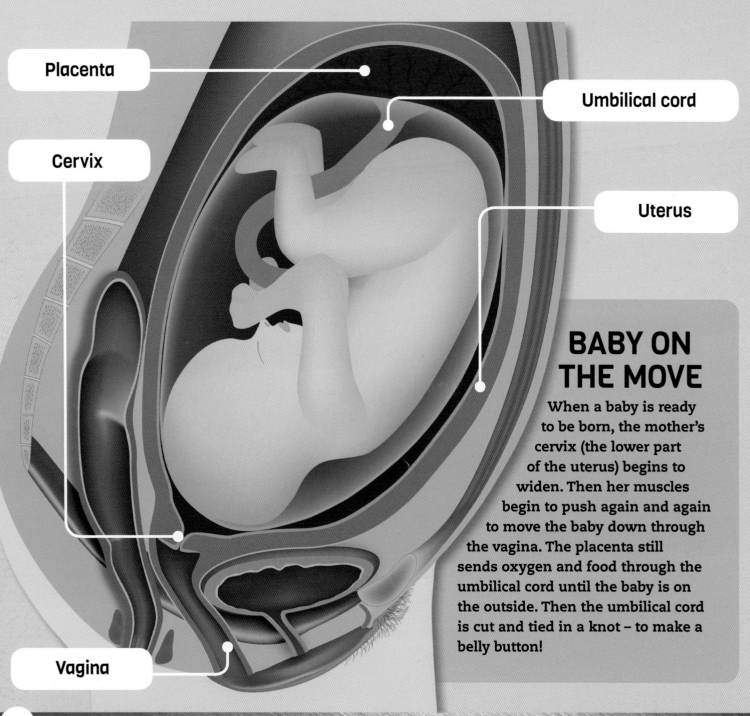

Placenta

Umbilical cord

Cervix

Uterus

Vagina

BABY ON THE MOVE

When a baby is ready to be born, the mother's cervix (the lower part of the uterus) begins to widen. Then her muscles begin to push again and again to move the baby down through the vagina. The placenta still sends oxygen and food through the umbilical cord until the baby is on the outside. Then the umbilical cord is cut and tied in a knot – to make a belly button!

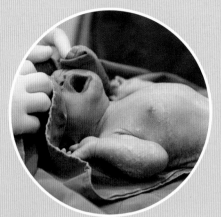

HAPPY BIRTHDAY!

The first sound you made was a loud cry. That wasn't because you were scared or unhappy. It was to try out your mouth, nose and lungs for breathing. For the past nine months, the umbilical cord has been doing that for you.

MOTHER'S MILK

Soon after being born, you would have been given your first feed, either from your mother's breast or from a bottle. Newborn babies cannot see very well, but they quickly learn to recognize their mother's smell, and find cuddling and feeding comforting. You would have been given all the food you needed through liquids until you were about six months old.

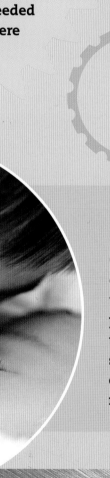

A NEW WORLD

Can you imagine experiencing everything for the first time? At first, the world would have been a confusing place to you. It takes babies a month or two before they can focus their eyes. Many scientists believe that babies' senses are confused at first – for example, they might 'hear' pictures, or 'see' music.

GROWING UP

You began growing the moment that your father's sperm fertilized your mother's egg. You're still growing now, and will continue to grow until you are about 18 or 19 years old. You go through lots of different stages of development before you become an adult. Then, as you head toward the middle of your life, you begin to notice signs that you're getting older.

2 years old
Confident on your feet

JOURNEY OF LIFE

As a child, you become aware of your body, and how the muscles all work together. When you're six months old, just being able to sit up is a big deal. Less than two years later, you're able to pedal a tricycle. You reach your full height by the time you're 20 years old. By your forties you are what is called middle-aged. Then, you reach old-age once you are around 75 years old.

8 years old
Growing about 5 cm (2 in) in a year

14 years old
Reaching puberty

25 years old
Peak physical condition

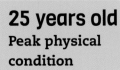

45 years old
'Middle age'

ON YOUR FEET!

You probably took your first steps when you were around a year old. You may have crawled first, then tried to stand up by holding on to things around you. By trial and error you learned what makes you trip or fall.

75 years old
Old age

BIG CHANGES

At about 12 years old, you hit a big change called puberty. This is when children begin the change into adults. You're still growing, but your body changes shape a little as you begin to resemble an adult. It's not just how you look that changes either. Girls' voices become a little deeper and boys' voices become much deeper.

BOYS

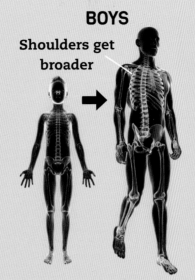

Shoulders get broader

Body becomes more hairy

GIRLS

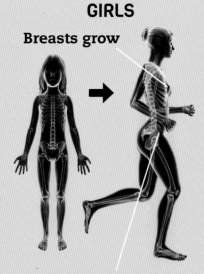

Breasts grow

Hips become wider

During the day, while you're standing up, the force of gravity pulls you down. So, each morning you wake up taller than when you went to sleep.

THE BALD TRUTH

One of the biggest clues that someone is reaching middle age is on the top of their head. Most men and women begin to get some silvery hairs, or maybe all of their hair turns that shade. Many men also lose some of their hair, usually from the front and top of their head.

SLOWING DOWN

Even the healthiest people begin to slow down as they enter old age. Their bodies can't recover from injury as well as before. Moving around takes more time because their muscles and bones aren't as strong.

YOU ARE UNIQUE

There are seven billion people alive in the world, but not a single one of them is exactly like you. Your body is different from anybody else's. That's just as well, because being able to prove who you are is important. Information about your unique body is called 'biometric' information. It can be used in all sorts of ways.

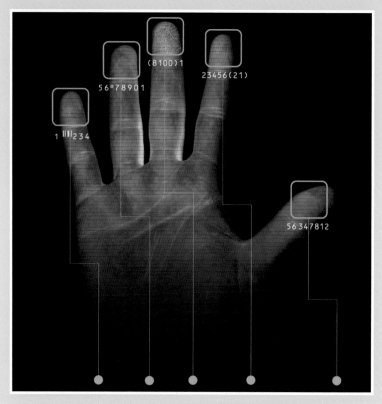

People can be identified from their fingerprints.

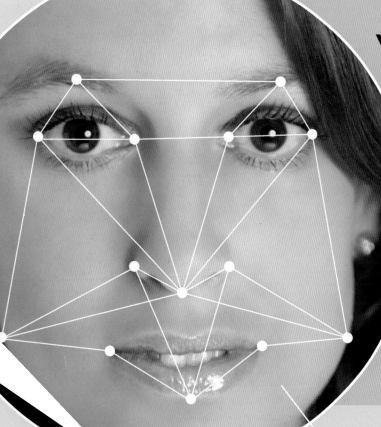

face recognition

YOUR ID, PLEASE?

Each year, large organizations find new ways to check people's identities. These checks are ways of stopping people from pretending they're you. A hundred years ago, a bank clerk would probably rely on recognizing your face if you wanted to take some money out of your account. Today, things are more advanced. Biometric identification can check different parts of your body, such as your hands and fingerprints (shown above) or face, with a camera or scanner to make sure it's really you. This kind of technology is even built into some modern phones.

SIGN ON THE DOTTED LINE

Some specialists are able to identify people by looking carefully at their handwriting. Is the writing big or small? Is it slanted or upright? Do all the letter "t's" look funny? Even if you try and disguise your writing, these experts believe they can identify you.

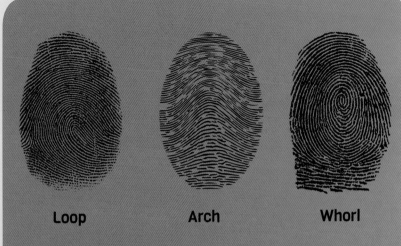

Loop   Arch   Whorl

WHORL LOT OF TROUBLE

Most people know that the police can check fingerprints to identify people. When you touch just about anything, you leave a print – even if you can't see it. That print is made by the patterns of little lines on each of your fingers. No two people have the same pattern of loops, whorls (spirals), and arches on their fingers.

Every person has a unique tongue print too!

ACTIVITY

You can "dust" a crime scene for prints! Put some cocoa powder into a cup. Dip a dry paintbrush into the powder and "dust" an area where there are fingerprints. Gently blow on the surface. Most of the powder will blow away, but some will stick to the grease of the fingerprints. Use a magnifying glass to find out: who did it?

A CODE FOR LIFE

Each of your body's trillions of cells contains a code. It's known as DNA, which is short for Deoxyribonucleic Acid. The "nucleic" in the middle of that big word tells you that the code is contained in the nucleus of each cell. This DNA code, or blueprint, guides the way cells grow, develop, and behave.

A TWIST OF FATE

DNA is a long, twisting molecule that is made up of four basic chemical building blocks – adenine, thymine, cytosine, and guanine. These form pairs inside the DNA. Each pair is like one rung of a long ladder, with a backbone holding those "rungs" in place. Although there are only four of these chemicals, they can be arranged to make many different combinations.

A gene is a length of DNA. Each cell in your body contains about 25,000 to 35,000 genes. These carry the information that makes you who you are. About 99.9 percent of the DNA of every person on the planet is exactly the same. It's the remaining 0.1 percent that makes each of us unique.

Because of the information in DNA, most people look a little like their parents. But not always!

IT'S IN THE GENES

Genes passed on to you from your parents determine many of your characteristics, known as traits. Inherited traits are ones you were born with and which you may pass on to your own children. They include whether you have blue or brown eyes. In fact, a scientist could look at your genes when you were a week old and have an idea about whether you will grow up to be tall or short, or whether you are likely to be good at sport or a talented artist.

NEW GENES

Sometimes, faulty genes can be passed on from parents to children, and can cause disease. Medical scientists are beginning to use "gene therapy" to prevent or treat some inherited diseases. One method involves replacing faulty genes with healthy ones.

DOUBLE TAKE

Have you ever wondered why identical twins are identical? It's because they've inherited exactly the same DNA. So if one of them has blond hair, the other one will. And if one of them has lots of freckles, the twin will also be covered in freckles. Unless you're an identical twin, your DNA is different from everyone else who has ever lived.

ALL PART OF THE FAMILY

As a human, you are a type of animal... and that means that you are related to other animals. You may not be covered in fur or scales, but you have a lot in common with many other creatures, especially apes.

FAMILY PORTRAIT

You're part of a large group of animals known as mammals. Like other mammals, including cats, elephants, and mice, you have hair. Also, you didn't hatch from an egg and you drank your mother's milk (or similar milk) when you were a baby.

NOT SO DIFFERENT

Your body shares its basic structure with other mammals. You have exactly the same organ systems as a dog, though your brain or heart may not be the same shape or size. A giraffe may have a long neck, but it has just the same number of neck bones as a human.

OUR CLOSEST RELATIVES

Some mammals are so closely related that they share more than 98 percent of their DNA with us. They are the four types of great apes – gorillas, orangutans, chimpanzees, and bonobos.

Some scientists call humans "the third chimpanzee" because two types of chimpanzee – the common chimpanzee and the bonobo – are so closely related to humans.

98.4 percent

of a human's genes are identical to those chimp genes.

WALKING TALL

Not everything about your body is the same as other apes, though. Walk a few steps and clap your hands at the same time. Easy – right? For humans, yes, but not for other apes. Chimpanzees and gorillas are on all fours a lot of the time. As a human, your bones are organized in a way that makes it easy for you to stand up.

FUEL FOR THE
BODY

Your body has to break down the food you eat in order to get the nutrients, which are the substances you need to keep healthy. This process is called digestion, and it begins the moment food enters your mouth. For your food, this is the start of a long journey. Along the way, your digestive system churns, pushes, squeezes, and breaks down the food until all of the nutrients are released into your body.

The process of digestion usually takes hours, although your body can process some foods and drinks more quickly. Your digestive system has many tools to get the job done efficiently – powerful chemicals, strong acids, expanding organs, and muscles that work continuously without you even realizing it!

OPEN WIDE

Which food do you like best? Is it ice cream or a juicy peach, chips, or a delicious pizza? Is your mouth watering even as you think about it? When your mouth starts to produce saliva (or spit) at the idea of something tasty, it's really getting ready to go to work!

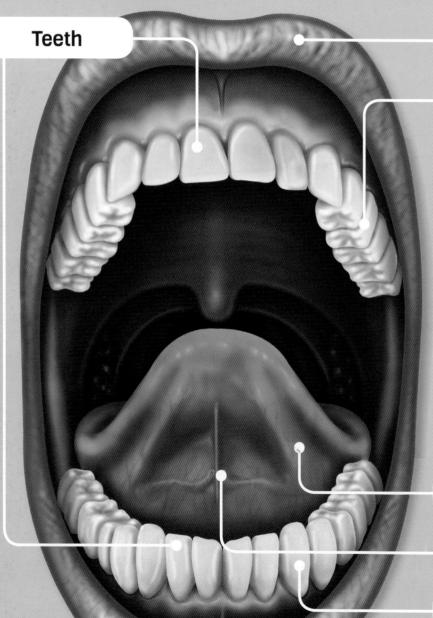

Teeth

Upper lip

Molars

FIRST STOP

First, your teeth cut and grind up your food. Depending on their shape and where they are in your mouth, your teeth do different jobs. Sharp, narrow teeth called incisors at the front of your mouth cut food into small bits. The wider molars towards the back of your mouth grind up these pieces of food. Your tongue stands guard, keeping the food near to your teeth until it's been fully chewed.

Tongue

Sublingual glands

Incisors

Lower lip

ACTIVITY

If you have jelly, or jello, for dessert, set a bowl aside. Mix in some pineapple or kiwi fruit and leave for ten minutes. You'll see that the gelatin has become liquid. That's because these fruits contain a chemical that breaks the gelatin down – just as your saliva breaks down the food in your mouth.

JUICY!

Saliva moistens your food and helps to make it mushy. It also helps to break down food that may be trapped between your teeth – so it helps prevent tooth decay as well. A nice smell, such as freshly baked bread, can sometimes "make your mouth water." That's because your senses of smell and taste are very closely linked.

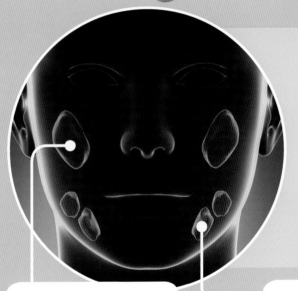

Parotid glands

Sublingual glands

SOAKING IT ALL UP

Saliva is made by glands in your mouth. These are the sublingual glands, which lie below the tongue, and the parotid glands at the back of your mouth. Food needs to be moist before it can be digested. Saliva does that job. It's made of water and other chemicals. One of those chemicals is called amylase, which starts to break down your food even before you swallow.

EASY TO SWALLOW

Once your food has been chewed and softened with saliva, your tongue rolls it into a ball, called a bolus. Then your tongue pushes this mushed-up bolus to the back of your mouth ready for the next stage in your food's digestive journey.

Your mouth contains more bacteria than the combined populations of the United States and Canada.

DOWN THE HATCH

You've chewed that tasty morsel and your tongue has rolled it into a ball. Now it's time to send it on its way to your stomach. But as it heads down your throat, there's a fork in the road: will it go straight to your stomach or wind up stuck in your windpipe?

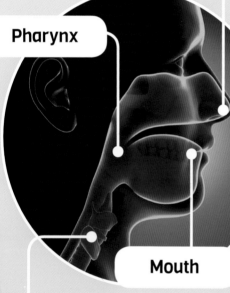

Nose

Pharynx

Mouth

Trachea (windpipe)

SIDE BY SIDE

The pharynx is the area at the back of your mouth that leads into your throat. It deals with both eating and breathing. Your food passes that way, as well as the air being breathed in through your nose. Your food heads down your throat, or gullet, to your stomach. Meanwhile, air passes through your trachea (windpipe) to your lungs. The openings to these two passageways are right next door to each other.

GONE THE WRONG WAY?

If you drink too quickly you may start to cough. That's because some of the liquid went down "the wrong way". When you swallow, a flap called the epiglottis stops liquid and food from entering your trachea. If your epiglottis doesn't close in time, some of the drink may go into your trachea. You automatically cough to send the liquid straight back out, so you don't choke!

SAFE SWALLOWING

You can't eat and breathe at the same time – it would mean keeping both your trachea and gullet open at the same time. And that would be a recipe for disaster! You'd choke because the food would block your breathing. But a clever bit of design means that just as you are about to swallow, your epiglottis folds down to cover the top of your trachea. So when you swallow, your food heads safely down your gullet.

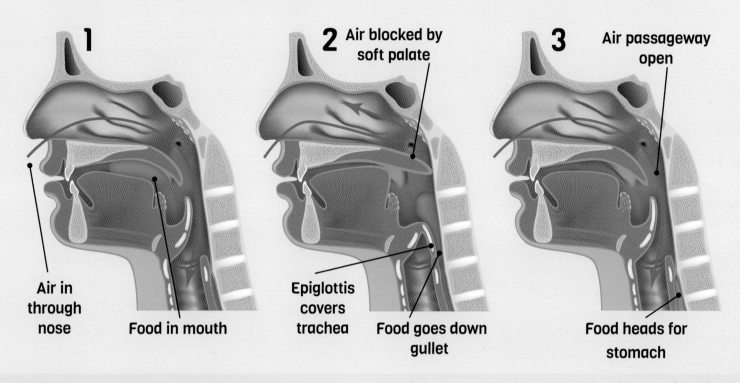

1
Air in through nose
Food in mouth

2 Air blocked by soft palate
Epiglottis covers trachea
Food goes down gullet

3 Air passageway open
Food heads for stomach

Burping is the way your body gets rid of air that you accidentally swallowed. In some countries, letting out a soft burp is a sign that you've enjoyed your food!

FEELING THE SQUEEZE

Food doesn't just drop down your gullet. Circular muscles around your gullet tighten behind the bolus of food and remain relaxed in front of it. This makes it easier for it to slide down. The process is called peristalsis. It's a bit like eating a frozen ice pop – you squeeze behind the ice to push it out the open end.

STOMACH CHURNING

Your food takes no more than ten seconds to pass through into your stomach. That's where the real process of digestion starts to happen. Your stomach is shaped like a letter J. It is one of the most important organs in your digestive system. A stomach is normally about the size of your fist, but it stretches and gets bigger as you fill it up with food.

GETTING TO WORK

All the work of mashing and churning the food happens in the body of your stomach. This is where those balls of food that come down your gullet get turned into a mushy liquid. The powerful muscles in the walls of your stomach squeeze the food. At the same time, the stomach wall produces enzymes and strong acids called gastric juices to break down the food further. After some squeezing and dissolving, the food turns into a liquid called chyme.

ACTIVITY

Take an old coin and put it in a glass filled with cola. Leave overnight. Next morning, rinse and remove the coin. It should be much shinier. That's because acid in the cola eats away at the layer of dirt on the coin. Acid in your stomach breaks down the food you eat in much the same way.

Cardiac sphincter

Gullet

Pylorus sphincter

Pyloric

Body of stomach

To small intestine

Powerful muscles

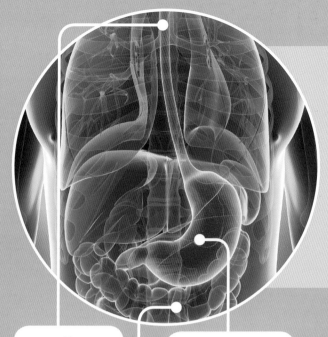

Gullet

Stomach

Small intestine

ONE-WAY SYSTEM

Your stomach is just one part of a whole series of different organs through which food passes as it's digested. Before entering the stomach, food travels down the gullet, and after leaving the stomach, it travels into the small intestine at the other end. Special valves called sphincters control the flow of food at each end. They make sure that food travels the right way through your body.

The acid in your stomach is strong enough to dissolve metal – but it wouldn't be a very tasty meal!

BELLY BALLOON

Your stomach expands just like a balloon as it fills with digested food.

BURNING UP

Sometimes, food and gastric juice from the stomach goes the wrong way through a sphincter, back into the gullet. Stomach acid in the base of the gullet causes heartburn – which can be very painful.

UNDER CONTROL

Special cells in your stomach wall (shown left) allow it to expand. They also control the balance of chemicals – so your stomach doesn't start to digest itself!

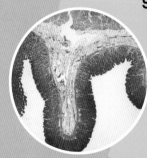

BIG AND SMALL

All that chewing, mushing, and acid treatment gets your food good and squishy by the time it leaves your stomach. It's now ready for the next stage of digestion – removing the nutrients and getting rid of what's not needed. And this is when the small and large intestines have their starring roles.

Stomach

Large intestine

Transverse colon

Ascending colon

Descending colon

Small intestine

Rectum

Anus

NOT SO SMALL!

Your mushed-up food leaves the stomach and enters the small intestine. The small intestine isn't really small – it's just narrower than the large intestine. The food spends around four hours working its way through the sections of this intestine. In the first bit – the duodenum – it gets broken down even further. In the second and third bits, nutrients and vitamins are absorbed into your body's bloodstream.

The small intestine is much longer than the large intestine! Uncoiled, it would stretch 6 m (20 ft). That's more than the height of three basketball players standing on each other's shoulders!

FINGER FOOD

The lining of the small intestine is covered with tiny, narrow shapes called villi (and even tinier microvilli). Through a powerful microscope, villi look like tiny fingers swaying gently as they stir up your food. Villi are very good at removing nutrients and passing them to the blood that's heading to the rest of your body. Some of the villi are only two cells thick – so nutrients can pass through them easily.

LAST CHANCE

The large intestine is your body's last chance to extract nutrients from what you ate hours before. But there's more going on than simply getting the last bits of goodness from the food mixture. Many different types of bacteria live in the large intestine. Some of them produce important vitamins and chemicals. These get absorbed into your bloodstream along with everything else.

EVERY LAST DROP

The large intestine is much shorter than the small intestine, but it's called "large" because it's wider. By the time your food moves into the large intestine, most of the important nutrients have been absorbed, but there's still some more to be collected – along with water. The food mixture (now mostly waste) is pretty dry when it moves through the descending colon into the rectum. And there it stays until you go to the toilet.

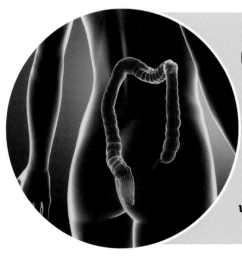

OUT YOU GO!

The rectum is the end of the line as far as your digestive system is concerned. It's like a storage room for waste – waiting there until you go to the toilet. And when you do, the waste is pushed out through peristalsis, the same way the food was pushed down your gullet. Sphincter muscles keep your anus – the real end of the line – tightly shut until you decide that you're ready to use the lavatory.

A BALANCED DIET

It's important to eat a healthy, balanced diet to give your body the wide range of nutrients it needs. It's fine to eat pizza or ice cream from time to time – as long as you eat lots of other healthy foods too!

WHAT YOUR BODY NEEDS:

BRAIN – You need magnesium (from leafy vegetables) and vitamin E (present in many nuts) to help the brain to function well.

MUSCLES – Protein (in meat, fish, nuts, and beans) helps build muscles.

BONES – Calcium (in most dairy products) keeps bones strong.

HAIR – Iron, vitamins A and C, protein, and zinc (from a range of foods) keep your hair strong and shiny.

HEART – Your heart is a muscle, so it has all of the requirements of a normal muscle.

SKIN – Vitamin E (in avocados and pine nuts) and the chemicals in many fruits help your skin.

FINGERNAILS – Zinc, protein, and some fatty acids (from oily fish) all keep your nails looking good.

IT'S GOOD FOR YOU!

The saying "you are what you eat" is surprisingly true. The minerals, vitamins, and other nutrients in your food are absorbed into your body, becoming part of it. Some help specific parts of your body, such as calcium in milk, which is excellent for building bones and teeth. Others help your whole body. Carbohydrates in pasta and rice give your body energy and keep you moving.

BRAIN FOOD?

For centuries, fish was known as "brain food". Was that just a myth? Scientists now agree that some fatty acids really do help the brain. And the food that contains these acids – actually it's fish!

SUPERFOODS?

Some people describe blueberries, pomegranate juice, garlic, broccoli, and other foods as "superfoods". They claim that these foods and drinks can help fight disease, keep you healthy, and even help you live longer. Scientists agree that while all these foods are good for you, they don't necessarily work miracles! Far more important is to eat a "super diet" – the balanced diet that gives your body the wide range of nutrients it needs to work well.

NAUGHTY BUT NICE!

Foods such as ice cream and pizza should be occasional treats. Most ice cream contains lots of fat and sugar, and pizza is heavy in fat. Although your body needs some fat in a balanced diet, it doesn't require a lot, and too much of the types of fats found in foods like sausages, cheese, or cookies can cause health problems.

Your body contains enough iron to make a spike large enough to hold your weight!

HELPFUL ALLIES

Many of your body's internal organs are found close to each other in your abdomen. That's the part of your body that's just above and below your belly button. The liver, pancreas, and gall bladder all play their part in helping you digest food.

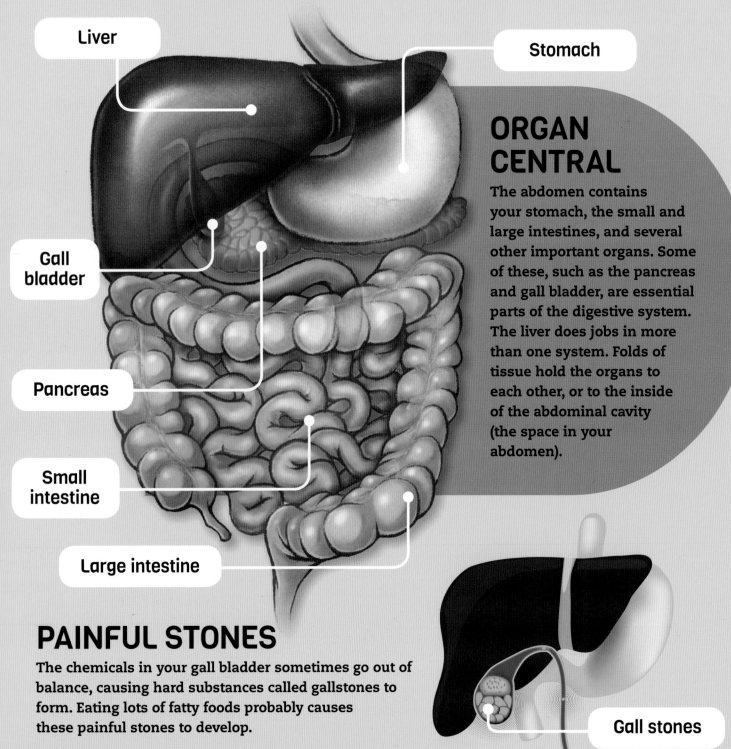

Liver

Stomach

Gall bladder

Pancreas

Small intestine

Large intestine

Gall stones

ORGAN CENTRAL

The abdomen contains your stomach, the small and large intestines, and several other important organs. Some of these, such as the pancreas and gall bladder, are essential parts of the digestive system. The liver does jobs in more than one system. Folds of tissue hold the organs to each other, or to the inside of the abdominal cavity (the space in your abdomen).

PAINFUL STONES

The chemicals in your gall bladder sometimes go out of balance, causing hard substances called gallstones to form. Eating lots of fatty foods probably causes these painful stones to develop.

INTO THE MIX

The pancreas makes substances called enzymes. These are used in your small intestine to break down carbohydrates, proteins, and fats. It also makes and sends a chemical called bicarbonate of soda to the small intestine. The bicarbonate of soda reacts with the acid in the intestine, stopping it from getting too strong and damaging the lining of the small intestine.

ACTIVITY

Put three teaspoons of bicarbonate of soda into an empty plastic bottle. Pour in a cup of vinegar and stretch a balloon across the top of the bottle. Soon, the balloon fills up. That's because the bicarbonate and vinegar (acid) react – just as bicarbonate and acid juices do in the intestine.

STAR PLAYER

If you were asked to name your most important organ, you would probably say your heart (pictured on the right). But after looking at the liver closely, you might think twice. The liver (shown below on the left) is your largest internal organ. It gives a final check to the blood coming from the digestive system – turning the nutrients into useful substances and filtering out any bad bits. It also produces bile, a liquid used to break down and digest fat.

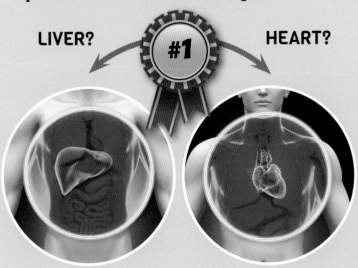

LIVER?   #1   HEART?

FIGHTING THE FAT

The bile produced by the liver is stored in the gall bladder. You need some fat in your diet because it stores energy for emergencies. So if the food arriving in the small intestine seems a bit fatty, the gall bladder squeezes out some bile. The bile breaks the fat down until it's ready to be absorbed by the body.

BLOOD CLEANING

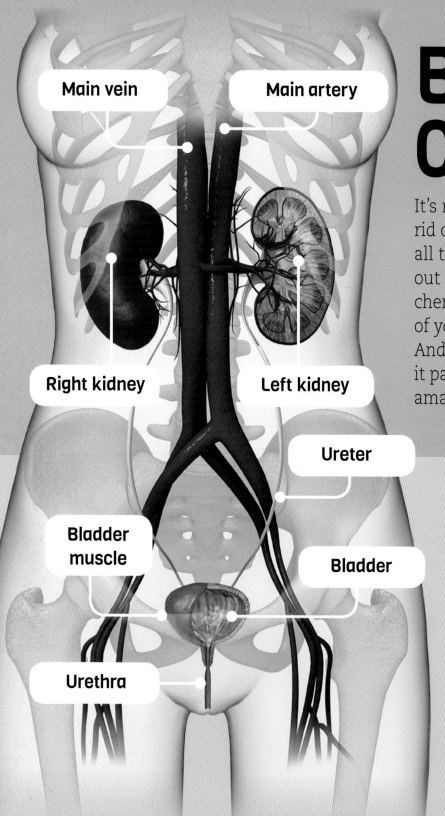

Main vein

Main artery

Right kidney

Left kidney

Ureter

Bladder muscle

Bladder

Urethra

It's really important for your body to get rid of the waste that it can't use. It sends all the solid waste from food down and out through your rectum. But all the chemical reactions going on in other parts of your body create even more waste. And that waste stays in your blood until it passes through another of your body's amazing systems – your kidneys.

CLEANING SYSTEM

Your body always has about 5 l (1.3 gallons) of blood flowing through it. The blood that leaves the digestive system is full of nutrients that are processed in other parts of the body. The chemical reactions that have processed the nutrients leave waste behind. So as the blood makes its way back to your heart, it passes through your two kidneys so it can be cleaned.

WATER WORKS

The kidneys filter your blood and the waste goes into a liquid, which is mostly water. This is called urine. The second part of the kidneys' job is to get rid of the urine, so the wastes don't remain in your body.

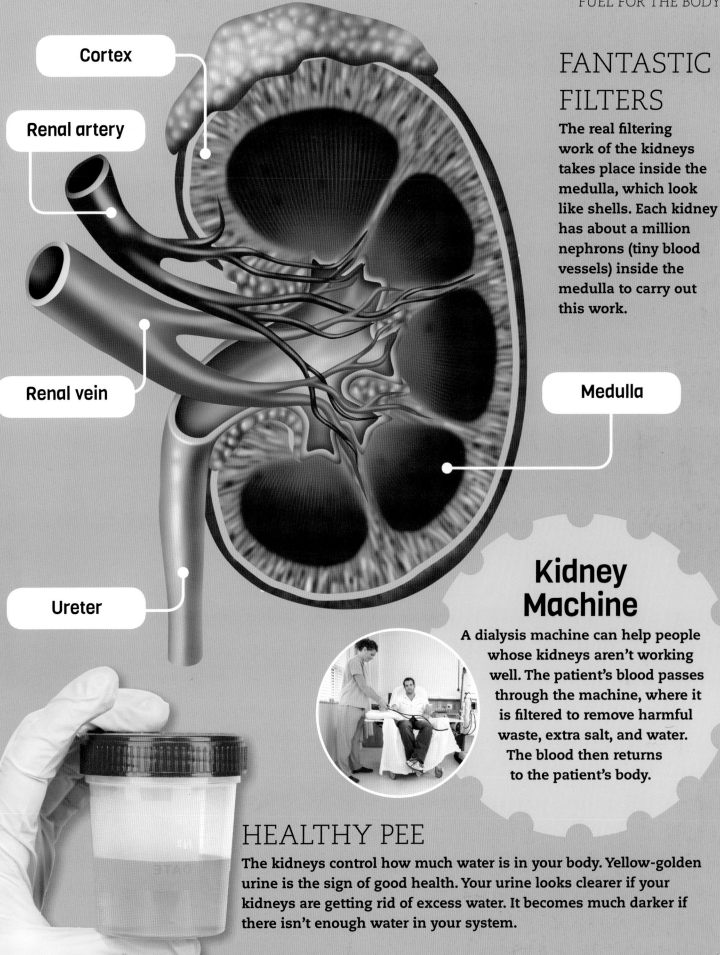

Cortex

Renal artery

Renal vein

Ureter

Medulla

FANTASTIC FILTERS

The real filtering work of the kidneys takes place inside the medulla, which look like shells. Each kidney has about a million nephrons (tiny blood vessels) inside the medulla to carry out this work.

Kidney Machine

A dialysis machine can help people whose kidneys aren't working well. The patient's blood passes through the machine, where it is filtered to remove harmful waste, extra salt, and water. The blood then returns to the patient's body.

HEALTHY PEE

The kidneys control how much water is in your body. Yellow-golden urine is the sign of good health. Your urine looks clearer if your kidneys are getting rid of excess water. It becomes much darker if there isn't enough water in your system.

CARBOHYDRATES
These break down into sugars that give you quick energy.

PROTEINS
The strength in your muscles is thanks to proteins.

FATS
These provide a "storehouse" for energy.

THE POWER STATION

The digestive system – working all the way from your teeth to your stomach and intestines – does a great job of extracting all the nutrients that your body needs. You've also done your bit by making sure that your diet includes a good balance of carbohydrates, proteins, and fats. So what happens to those nutrients once they've been sent off from the intestines?

GOOD NUTRITION

Your body needs a wide range of nutrients. The "big three" group of nutrients are carbohydrates, proteins, and fats. Some foods contain lots of one group. For example, a steak is high in protein and butter has lots of fat. But your overall diet should be a balance between them. A chicken sandwich is a good example of food that provides some of all three: the bread has carbohydrates, the chicken supplies protein, and the butter supplies the fat.

During a match, tennis players often eat bananas. They are easy to digest and are high in carbohydrates, which the body uses to produce energy.

POWER UP

Proteins in food are broken down into pieces called amino acids. Your body then puts the amino acids back together to make different proteins that carry out special jobs. These new proteins help other chemical reactions, help cells to communicate with each other, and even provide energy if there isn't enough carbohydrate or fat.

BREAKING THINGS DOWN

To release energy and keep you moving, your body uses chemical reactions to break down carbohydrates and fats. The bonds that hold some molecules together contain lots of energy, and breaking them apart releases that energy. This breaking down of bonds is called the catabolic process.

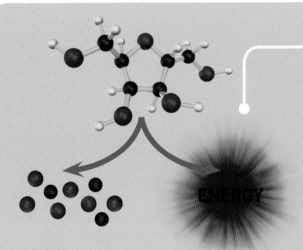

ENERGY

BUILDING THINGS UP

The opposite of the catabolic process is the anabolic process. Your body works with smaller molecules to produce larger ones. In this way it also builds new proteins.

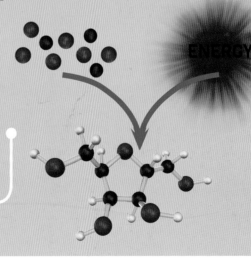

ENERGY

AN ACTIVE YOU!

Together with a good, balanced diet, exercise helps to keep your body running smoothly. Taking some exercise, such as playing sport or going to a gym, also helps you to stay at a healthy weight.

Lungs
Breathing deeply helps the lungs stay strong

Muscles
Regular exercise strengthens muscles

Waistline
Energy needed for exercise burns some of the fat stored around your waist

Joints
Exercise keeps joints moving well

During your lifetime, you will eat about 27,000 kg (60,000 lb) of food – about the weight of six elephants!

BURNING CALORIES

A "calorie" is a unit used to measure the energy stored in food and in your body. When you eat, the calories in food are turned into energy. If you eat more calories than your body needs for energy, those extra calories get stored as fat. Your body uses up calories just breathing, moving, and thinking! But when you exercise, you need more energy, so your body burns up some of the calories stored as fat.

Heart
Exercise gives your heart a good workout – after all, it's a muscle too

ACTIVITY

There are 97 calories in 25 g (1 oz) of sugar. Look at the small print on a cola can, or chocolate bar to see how much sugar it contains. Then, work out how many calories the sugar adds up to. Sugar should make up only 10 percent of your daily calorie intake - which for adults is around 2,200 calories!

Answers (clockwise from left): roast chicken 171 calories; banana 95 calories; fries 253 calories; strawberries 28 calories; pork sausages 305 calories; broccoli 24 calories; celery 7 calories; apple 47 calories; baked potato 109 calories.

HOW MANY CALORIES?

There are 95 calories in 100 g (4 oz) of banana. Guess how many calories there are in 100 g (4 oz) of these foods. Answers are on the right.

Pork sausages

Banana

Fries

Broccoli

Strawberries

Apple

Roast chicken

Baked potato

Celery

READY FOR
ACTION

Your body needs support to keep you upright. Your bones provide that support, linking up in a framework called your skeleton. They need to be strong enough to carry your weight, but light enough to help you stay active. Without your bones, your body would just flop down like a rag doll.

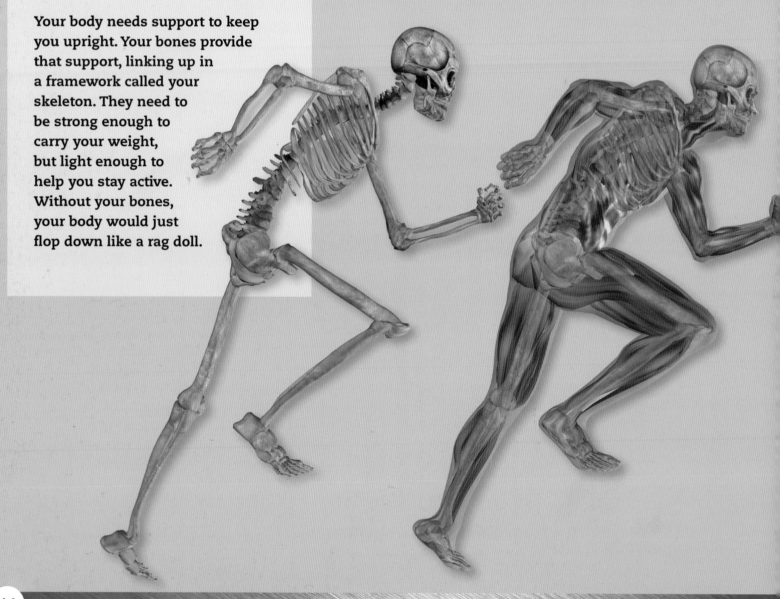

It's one thing being able to stand upright, but you also need a system to hold your bones together and to guide them. That's the job of your muscles. You call on them every time you need to move – whether it's picking up a piece of paper or running in a race. Behind the scenes are other muscles that work day and night – automatically – to keep your body functioning.

Your skin does more than just cover your body like a huge sheet of wrapping paper. It keeps you warm or cools you down, and it acts like a cushion to protect what's inside. It's waterproof and it protects you from the sun's most harmful rays.

THE SKELETON CREW

Your skeleton is your body's framework – a scaffolding of bones that gives you support, just as strong metal girders support a skyscraper. Your bones give your body its shape and structure.

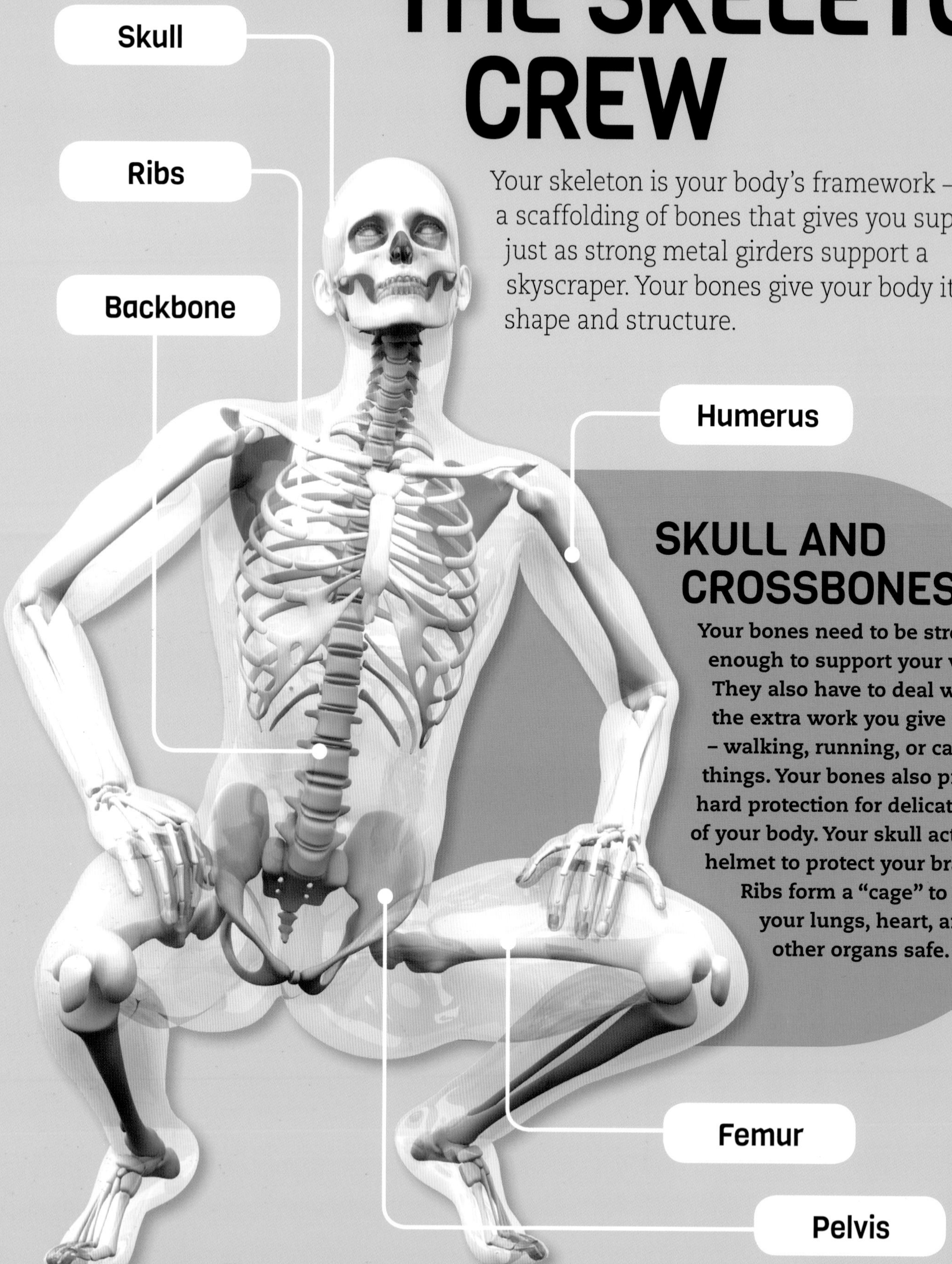

Skull

Ribs

Backbone

Humerus

SKULL AND CROSSBONES

Your bones need to be strong enough to support your weight. They also have to deal with the extra work you give them – walking, running, or carrying things. Your bones also provide hard protection for delicate parts of your body. Your skull acts as a helmet to protect your brain. Ribs form a "cage" to keep your lungs, heart, and other organs safe.

Femur

Pelvis

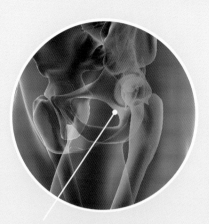

Ball-and-socket joint

JOINT ACTION

Joints are the junctions where your bones meet. Some are fixed, which means that the bones on either side stay in place. Others, like the elbow and knee, are called hinge joints. They move like the hinge of a door. Ball-and-socket joints at your shoulder and hip allow one of the bones to move much more freely – almost in any direction.

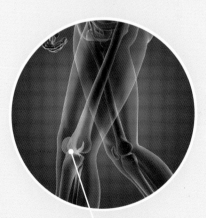

Hinge joint

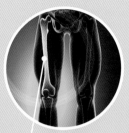

Femur

Stapes

BIG AND SMALL

The femur, the long bone in your upper leg, is the largest bone in your body. It needs to be that big because it absorbs most of the force when you walk or run, or even stand. The smallest bone in your body is the stapes. It's only as big as a grain of rice and is found inside your ear. The stapes is one of a series of bones that picks up vibrations in the air and helps us to hear sounds.

Your ribs move each time you breathe. That's 5 million times each year!

FUNNY BONE

If you bang your elbow, it can give a sharp, stinging pain called "hitting your funny bone". But what's hurting is a nerve called the ulnar nerve. Most nerves are protected beneath bones and muscles, but this nerve is close under your skin by your elbow.

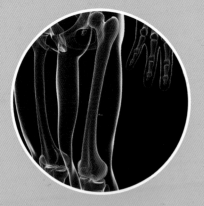

Flat bone (parietal bone in skull)

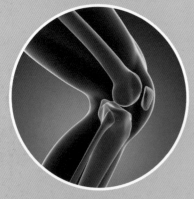

Long bone (femur)

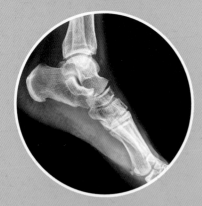

Sesamoid bone (patella)

Short bone (foot)

THE HARD STUFF

Your bones need to be very strong to stand up to the stresses they will meet throughout your lifetime. They also have to be light enough so you can move freely around. But your bones are not the hardest parts of your body – it's actually your teeth.

SHAPE UP!

When you were born, you started out with about 300 bones in your body. Some of those fuse, or join, together to become larger bones. An adult ends up with 206 bones. These bones have a spongy inside, called marrow, and a hard outside made of a chemical called calcium carbonate. What a bone does plays a part in how it's shaped. For example, flat bones are excellent protectors. Long bones support your moving limbs. Sesamoid bones help the junctions, or joints, between other bones. Short bones give you support without actually moving.

BLOOD FACTORY

Bones do more than just support and protect you. There is spongy marrow inside your bones which acts like a factory. Marrow produces blood cells that your body uses for energy, to fight disease, and to help you heal.

Marrow in a hip bone

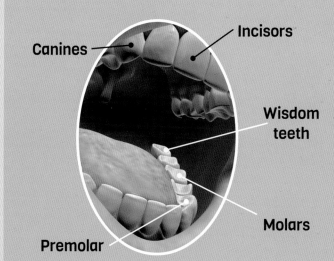

Canines — Incisors

Wisdom teeth

Molars

Premolar

THE DAILY GRIND

If want to see the hardest bits of your body, then just look in the mirror and smile! Throughout your lifetime, your teeth will cut and grind their way through thousands of meals. Like bones, their shape depends on their job. Incisors and canine teeth cut and tear food into smaller bits. Premolars and molars grind that food. Wisdom teeth are an extra set of molars that come out when you're around 20 years old.

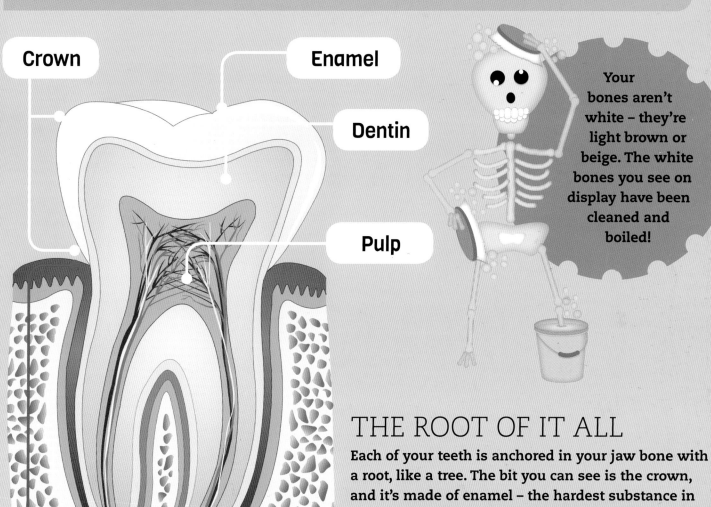

Crown

Enamel

Dentin

Pulp

Root

Your bones aren't white – they're light brown or beige. The white bones you see on display have been cleaned and boiled!

THE ROOT OF IT ALL

Each of your teeth is anchored in your jaw bone with a root, like a tree. The bit you can see is the crown, and it's made of enamel – the hardest substance in your whole body. Enamel protects the tooth from wear and tear. The layer below the enamel, dentin, is a bit softer, and it carries some nerves and blood. The pulp has most of the nerves and it sends signals to your brain, such as a painful toothache – ouch!

MEAT ON THE BONES

Muscles are the parts of your body that let you move around when you stand up, lift a box, or kick a ball. You can consciously tell some muscles what to do, but that is only part of the picture. Muscles also help to digest your food, make your heart beat, and make you breathe. You don't need to consciously tell those muscles what to do.

MOVE IT!

Your skeleton is the framework that keeps your body supported, and your muscles allow that framework to move. The type of muscles that move bones about are called voluntary muscles. First, you think about what movements you want to make. Then, your brain works out which muscles are needed and sends messages to those muscles. The muscles move, and so do you!

Muscles make up **40%** of your body weight.

40%

Wide-eyed

Muscles also help you see. Smooth muscles in your eyes work constantly to focus on whatever we want to look at. They close up the pupil in bright light and open it up in dim light. They react faster than any other muscle in the body.

There are more than
600 muscles
in your body! These range from the large gluteus maximus muscle in your rear end, to the tiny stapedius muscle in your ear.

stapedius
actual size

✗ ACTIVITY

Dim the lights. After a few minutes, look at your eyes in a mirror. You'll see that the pupils in the middle of your eyes are bigger. Brighten the lights and look again. They should be smaller. Your eye muscles have contracted, or shrunk, to keep out the bright light.

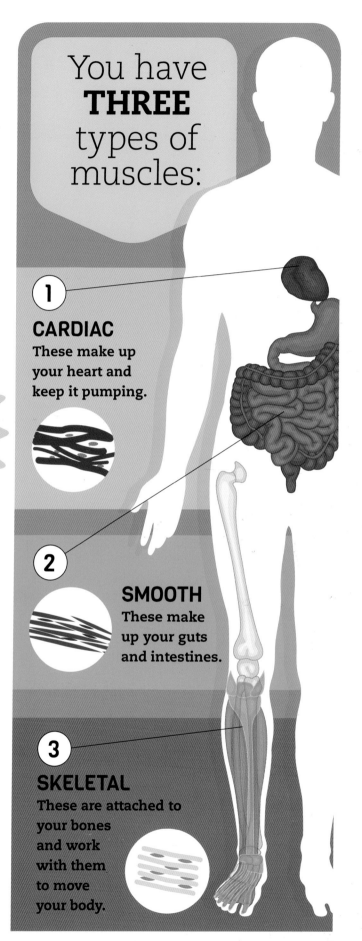

You have **THREE** types of muscles:

1

CARDIAC
These make up your heart and keep it pumping.

2

SMOOTH
These make up your guts and intestines.

3

SKELETAL
These are attached to your bones and work with them to move your body.

MUSCLE POWER

When you think of your muscles, you probably think about the ones you use to kick a football, hold a pen, or ride a bike. Those are your voluntary muscles, the ones that you can direct. They're also called skeletal muscles because they are connected to your bones.

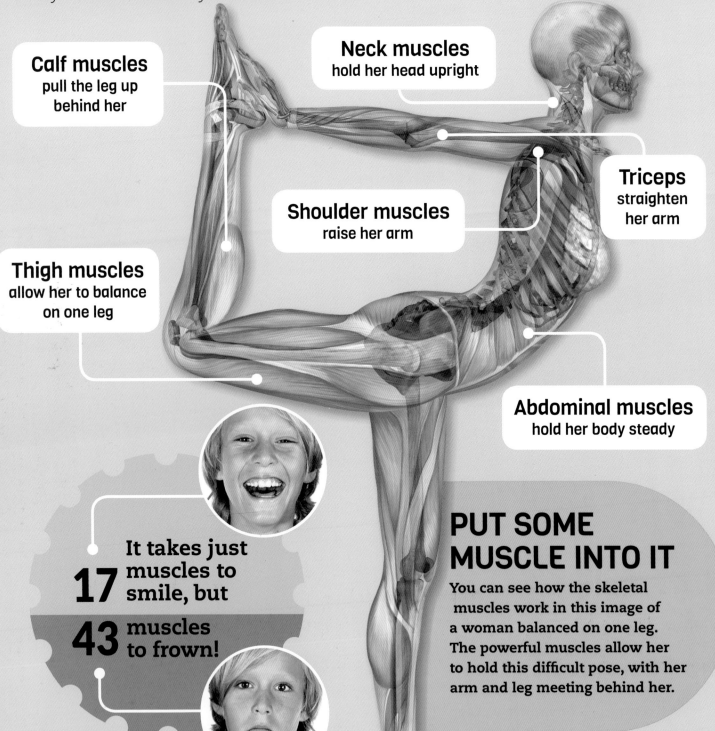

Calf muscles
pull the leg up behind her

Neck muscles
hold her head upright

Triceps
straighten her arm

Shoulder muscles
raise her arm

Thigh muscles
allow her to balance on one leg

Abdominal muscles
hold her body steady

It takes just **17** muscles to smile, but **43** muscles to frown!

PUT SOME MUSCLE INTO IT

You can see how the skeletal muscles work in this image of a woman balanced on one leg. The powerful muscles allow her to hold this difficult pose, with her arm and leg meeting behind her.

WORKING IN PAIRS

Muscles work in pairs that pull in opposite directions. They never push. Muscles contain a protein called actin. When another protein, myosin, sends a message to the actin, the muscle tightens up, or contracts. So when you show off and flex your arm muscles, it's the biceps muscle on the top side of your arm that pulls your lower arm up. When you straighten your arm, the triceps muscle on the other side pulls it back down again.

If all the muscles in your body pulled in one direction, you'd be able to lift

25 tons!

That's the weight of a whale!

ACTIVITY

Hold your right arm straight out in front of you. Count how many times you can open and close your fist in thirty seconds. Now, rest for fifteen seconds and try it again. The second number should be smaller because your muscles will be tired out!

BREATHING HARD

Muscles use oxygen from your blood supply to get energy. Normal blood flow allows you to continue with steady exercise, such as walking. But if you're more active, your muscles need more energy, and use up more oxygen. That's one of the reasons why you breathe harder when you exercise – your body is trying to get more oxygen.

WORKING NON-STOP

Your voluntary muscles sometimes get to take a break. For example, your tennis match might have ended or you've just finished the last lap in the pool. But there are other muscles in your body that are constantly working. They are your involuntary muscles, which keep your body ticking over. Cardiac muscles have kept your heart beating since the day you were born, and smooth muscles work with lots of organs inside your abdomen.

You don't control your involuntary muscles. The ciliary muscle in your eyes works automatically to help you to focus on objects both near and far!

W
EH
AVE
REMO
VEDAL
LTHERU
DEWORDS

Smooth muscles contract and relax constantly in the iris of your eye

ON DUTY 24/7

Involuntary muscles work all of the time, even when you're asleep. They work inside your body and help your body's systems to remain on duty for 24 hours of the day!

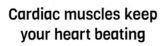

Cardiac muscles keep your heart beating

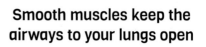

Smooth muscles keep the airways to your lungs open

ABDOMINAL WORKOUT

The muscles in your abdomen are pretty amazing! Not only do they protect your internal organs, but they also help you to breathe, and support your spine. The ones that help you swallow and digest food are called smooth muscles. They don't have the striped look of the much stronger voluntary or cardiac muscles (see page 51). There's an advantage to this smoothness. These muscles can squeeze and stretch in all different directions.

Lining of intestine

Smooth muscles

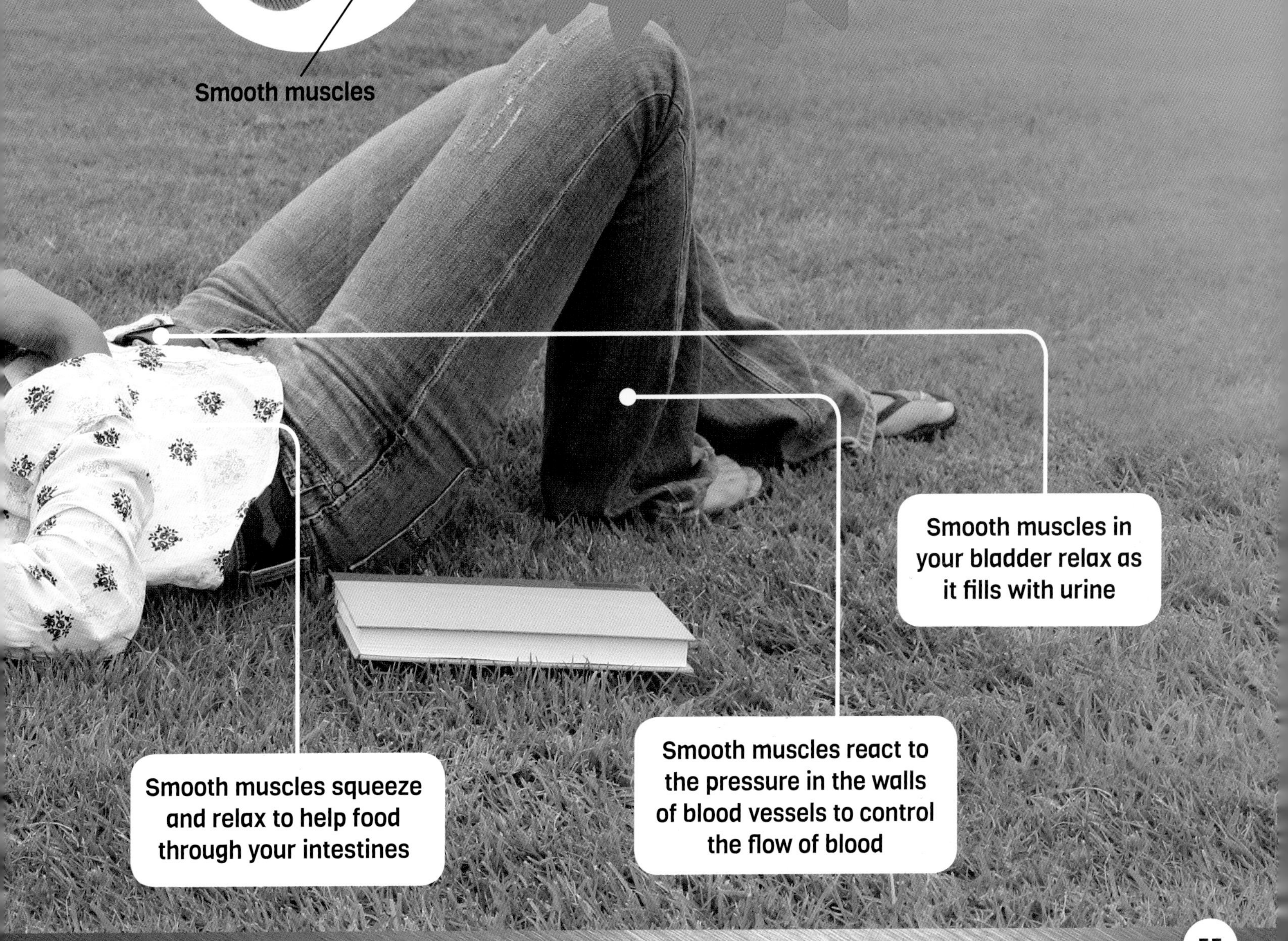

Smooth muscles in your bladder relax as it fills with urine

Smooth muscles react to the pressure in the walls of blood vessels to control the flow of blood

Smooth muscles squeeze and relax to help food through your intestines

TYING IT ALL TOGETHER

It's one thing having a skeleton to keep you upright. And it's another to have a set of muscles to move those bones around. But you need a few more elements to tie those systems together and make them work smoothly. That's the job of your cartilage, ligaments, and tendons.

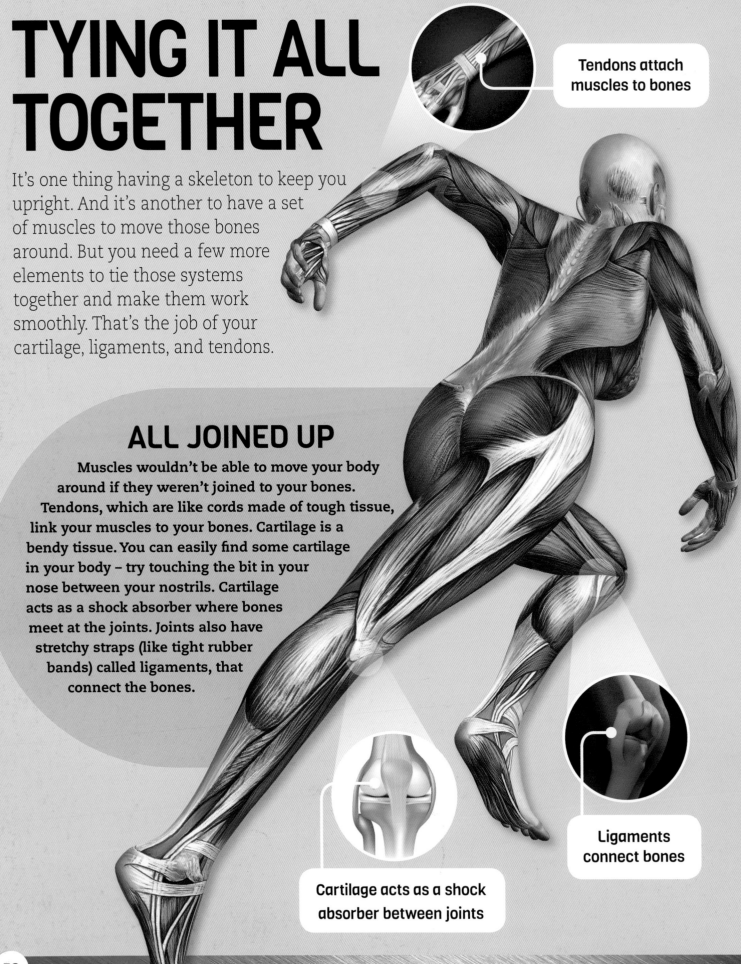

Tendons attach muscles to bones

ALL JOINED UP

Muscles wouldn't be able to move your body around if they weren't joined to your bones. Tendons, which are like cords made of tough tissue, link your muscles to your bones. Cartilage is a bendy tissue. You can easily find some cartilage in your body – try touching the bit in your nose between your nostrils. Cartilage acts as a shock absorber where bones meet at the joints. Joints also have stretchy straps (like tight rubber bands) called ligaments, that connect the bones.

Cartilage acts as a shock absorber between joints

Ligaments connect bones

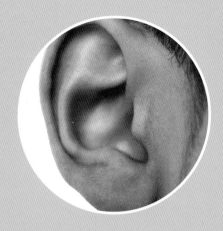

BEND AND STRETCH

Cartilage moves easily. That's why you can bend your ears (which are made mostly of cartilage) without hurting them. Cartilage is a good cushion to nestle between bones because it's soft. Your bones started as cartilage (see page 48). As you grew, new cartilage formed at the ends of your bones. That cartilage itself turned to bone, getting longer and longer, until you finally stop growing.

A human tendon is strong enough to hold a small car without tearing!

ACTIVITY

Fold your hands so that your fingers cross over each other. Then, straighten the ring finger (next to the pinkie) of each hand so their tips touch. Ask a friend to put a coin between these fingertips. Now, try to pull those fingers apart. You can't – because your tendons are pulling in the opposite direction.

CLOSE CONNECTIONS

Ligaments are short bands of tough, fibrous tissue. They connect bones to other bones to form a joint. They also prevent some joints from moving too freely. If you've ever twisted your ankle, you'll know what it's like to have a joint that moves too much.

SKIN DEEP

You probably think that your skin is just... well, skin. The important stuff is all inside, and the skin is the packaging, like the plastic wrapper on a new birthday card. However, your "birthday suit" is one of the busiest parts of your body – a waterproof, living coat that protects you.

Hair shaft

Epidermis

Dermis

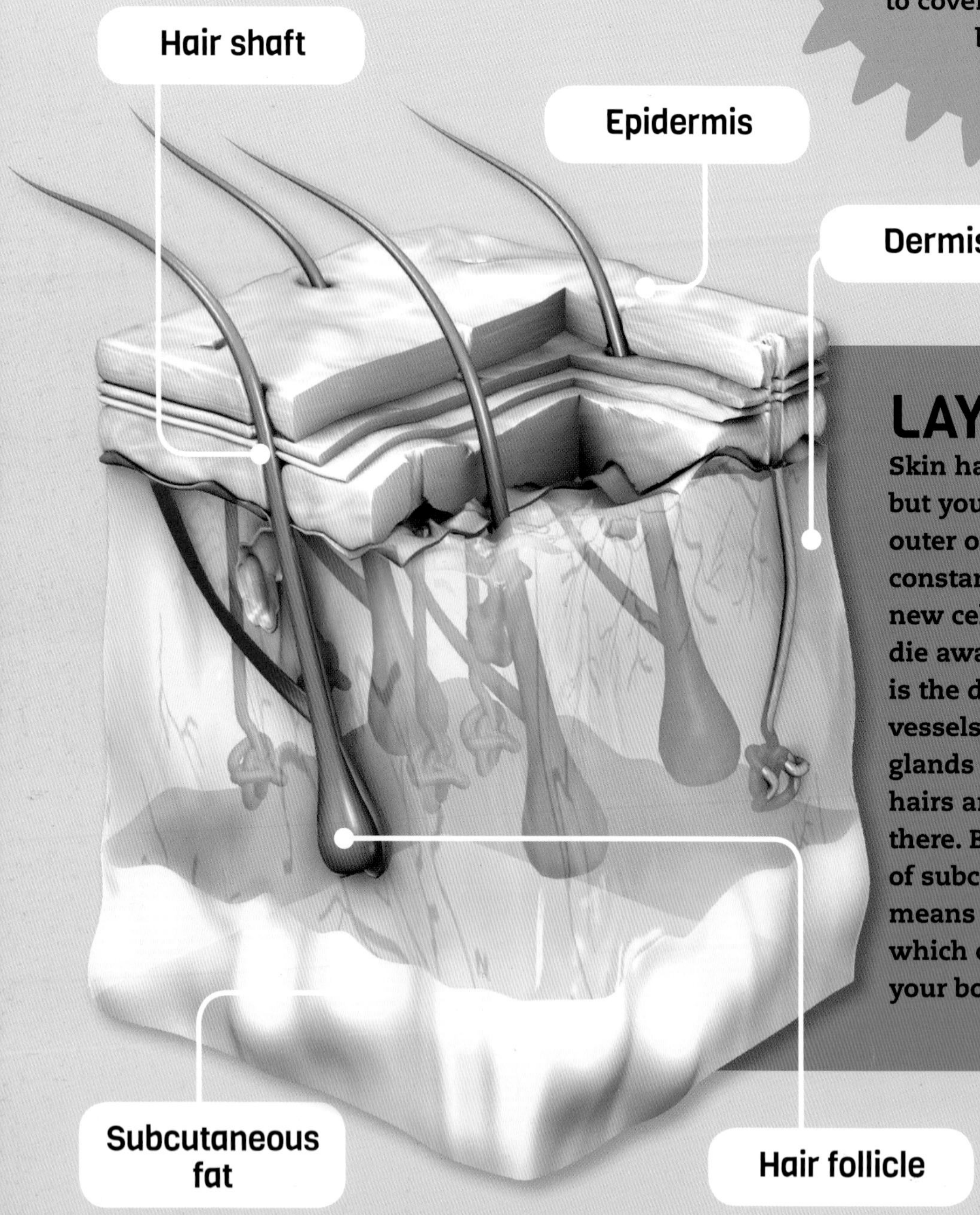

LAYERS

Skin has three layers, but you can only see the outer one, the epidermis. It's constantly at work, producing new cells to replace those that die away. Beneath the epidermis is the dermis, which has blood vessels such as capillaries. Sweat glands and hair follicles (where hairs are anchored) are also found there. Below the dermis is a layer of subcutaneous (which simply means "below the skin") fat, which cushions and keeps your body warm.

Subcutaneous fat

Hair follicle

COOLING DOWN

Have you ever seen steam rise or evaporate from a surface? The water has turned from a liquid to a gas. It's the same when you exercise. Your body produces a liquid called sweat through the tiny pores on your skin. As it becomes a gas, the sweat evaporates, taking some of the heat with it as it leaves your body – so you start cooling down.

FRECKLED SKIN

Your skin produces a substance called melanin to protect you from the sun's harmful rays. That's why your skin darkens if it's exposed to the sun. Sometimes, that extra melanin clumps up instead of being spread around, which is why some people get freckles. Although your skin does protect you up to a point, it's important to wear plenty of sunscreen as further protection from the sun.

WARMING UP

Your skin can "shut the door" on sweat pores as easily as it opens them. Your body produces extra heat when you begin to shiver in the cold. Shutting your sweat pores is a way of keeping that heat inside you!

Scientists can grow new skin from a small sample of human skin. The skin from one hand can produce enough skin to cover

36 Olympic swimming pools!

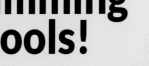

TOUGH AS NAILS

Did you know that not every part of your body is alive? Your hair and nails – at least, the parts that you can see – are made from dead cells. They are formed from a tough protein called keratin, which is also found in the hooves and horns of animals. They do not contain any nerve endings, which is why you can cut them.

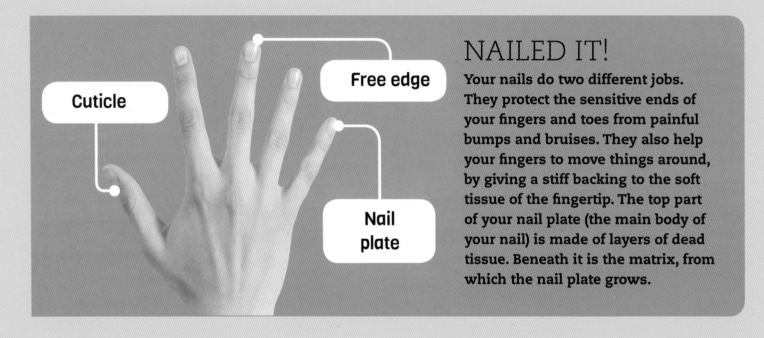

Cuticle

Free edge

Nail plate

NAILED IT!

Your nails do two different jobs. They protect the sensitive ends of your fingers and toes from painful bumps and bruises. They also help your fingers to move things around, by giving a stiff backing to the soft tissue of the fingertip. The top part of your nail plate (the main body of your nail) is made of layers of dead tissue. Beneath it is the matrix, from which the nail plate grows.

Fingernails grow four times faster than toenails!

STOP CHEWING YOUR CLAWS!

Why do you have nails and not claws at the ends of your fingers? You can thank your tree-climbing ancestors, the apes. Their claws shrank into nails to give their fingertips more of a feel for the safety of thin branches.

KEEPING A COOL HEAD

The type of hair you have is all down to your genes (see pages 20–21). In the same way that people have light or dark skin depending on where their ancestors lived, hair-types are also linked to sunlight and heat. Curly hair protects the head from the sun's harmful rays better than straight hair. It also allows air to move through it easily, helping you to keep cool.

Hair

Beard

SPOT THE SIMILARITIES

We are not the only animals with hair. Mammals have developed fur as a way of stopping their warm bodies from losing heat in cold weather. Like other apes, we don't have much hair on our faces. A chimpanzee, like many human males, has head hair, body hair, and a beard.

Fingernails

Chest hair

Toenails

HAIR TODAY...

Your hair starts down in the hair follicles, which are in the dermis (the layer of skin beneath the epidermis). New cells are constantly created, pushing older ones out and up. A layer of keratin (the same substance as your nails) forms around these dead cells, which gets pushed further out. Some men's hair follicles shrink over time, meaning no hair gets pushed out... and they begin to go bald.

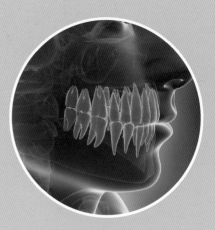

WISDOM TEETH

Humans once needed these extra teeth to chew roots and raw meat

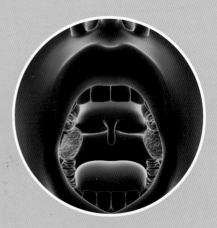

TONSILS

These help to fight infections, but you can manage without them.

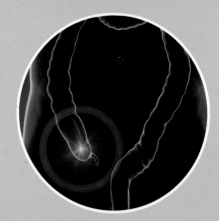

APPENDIX

Scientists used to think this organ was useless. Now we know it can help kill germs in your gut.

SPARE PARTS?

If you think of your body as a machine, then there must be some spare parts. These are the bits that don't get used so often, even if they once served a real purpose. That's because, over millions of years, human beings have changed or evolved.

NO JOB TO DO

Why do men have nipples? After all, they can't breastfeed babies. The reason is that we all develop in the same way in the first few weeks in the womb... and we are all following the instructions for being female. It's only after a few weeks that boys start to follow different, "male" instructions. By that time, everyone has nipples... and boys and men keep them, even though they have no job to do.

BLASTS FROM THE PAST

Other parts of your body, such as your tailbone (coccyx), appendix, and wisdom teeth, are reminders of how we may have looked and lived millions of years ago. Back then we were hunting mammoths, chewing raw plants, and climbing trees. You can think of them as fascinating links with the past.

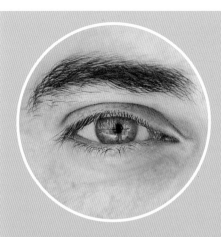

EYEBROW SLEUTH

Here's a chance to play medical detective. Why do you have eyebrows? And why might human beings have needed them in the past? One theory is that they stop sweat flowing into your eyes from your forehead. Another is that they are important for communicating emotions to people around you. What do you think?

ONE BIG HEADACHE?

Some bits of your body remain a mystery, and no one is really sure what they were ever meant to do – even in the distant past. Your sinuses are a good example. They're the hollow bits in your head behind your nose and cheeks. They can give you a terrible headache if they get infected, but no one knows for sure why you have them. The latest theory is that sinuses stop your head from being too heavy – because air weighs less than bone!

The coccyx is the lowest part of your backbone. It's the remains of a tailbone from our distant ancestors!

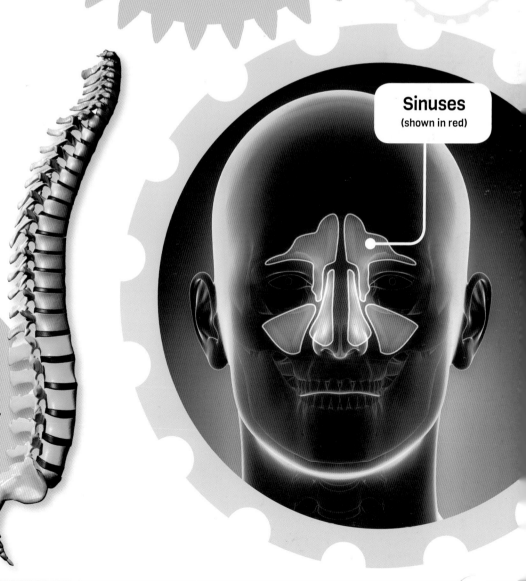

Sinuses
(shown in red)

LIFE SUPPORT

Your lungs and heart are always working, even while you sleep. Your lungs take in a gas called oxygen from the air. Meanwhile, your heart pumps blood to every part of your body. That blood contains oyxgen which it gets from your lungs. Without oxygen, your body would not work properly.

Chilling Out

When you exercise, your lungs and heart get to work immediately. You breathe harder and your heart beats much faster. This is so that more oxygen can reach your muscles to keep your body moving. As you get fitter, your body starts to work much harder and for longer.

WORKING OUT

FREAKING OUT

A shock or a fright can make you breathe quicker and your heart beat faster. This "fight or flight" response is your body's way of helping you to survive scary situations by preparing you for intense physical action. So, when you're afraid, your lungs take in air faster to supply your blood with oxygen, and your heart beats faster so it can pump more blood to your muscles.

HAVE A HEART

Your heart is about the size of your fist and it has a very important job to do. It pumps blood that's full of oxygen hard and fast enough to reach every part of your body. Nothing would work without that oxygen-rich blood, so your heart really is an important organ.

BODY PUMP

Your heart sits in the middle of your chest, protected by your ribs. It is close to your lungs and works like a pump. Before each heartbeat, your heart fills up with blood. Then, it squeezes sharply – which is the beat – to send blood squirting away to other parts of your body. Did you know your heart beats about 100,000 times in one day and about 35 million times in a year. That's pretty amazing!

ACTIVITY

Ask a friend to put their two first fingers lightly down on your inner wrist. When they feel a pulse, ask them to count it while you time them for 15 seconds. Multiply the result by four to get your pulse rate (beats per minute).

DISTANT DRUMS

You can feel your heartbeat by putting your hand on your chest. But the beats are strong enough to be felt well away from your heart. You can feel them by checking your pulse. Place your hand just above one of your larger arteries (which carry blood from the heart). One pulse is on the side of your neck. Another is on the inside of your wrist.

HEART AT WORK

Your heart is made up of four chambers: left atrium, right atrium, left ventricle, and right ventricle. The right side receives deoxygenated blood (blood in which the oxygen has been used up) from the body and sends it to the lungs, where oxygen is added. The left side takes the blood from the lungs and pumps it to the rest of your body. Deoxygenated blood arrives at the heart through blood vessels called veins, while oxygenated blood leaves the heart through blood vessels called arteries. Valves in the heart stop blood from flowing in the wrong direction.

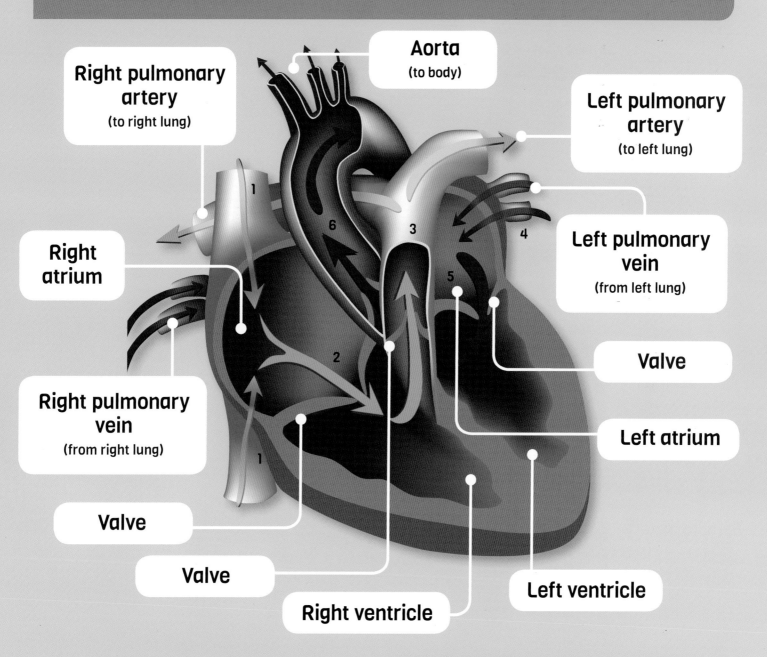

Aorta (to body)

Right pulmonary artery (to right lung)

Left pulmonary artery (to left lung)

Right atrium

Left pulmonary vein (from left lung)

Right pulmonary vein (from right lung)

Valve

Valve

Left atrium

Valve

Left ventricle

Right ventricle

1 Blood from body into the heart

2 Blood from right atrium to right ventricle

3 Blood from right ventricle to lungs

4 Oxygen-rich blood from lungs into left atrium

5 Oxygen-rich blood into left ventricle

6 Oxygen-rich blood out to body

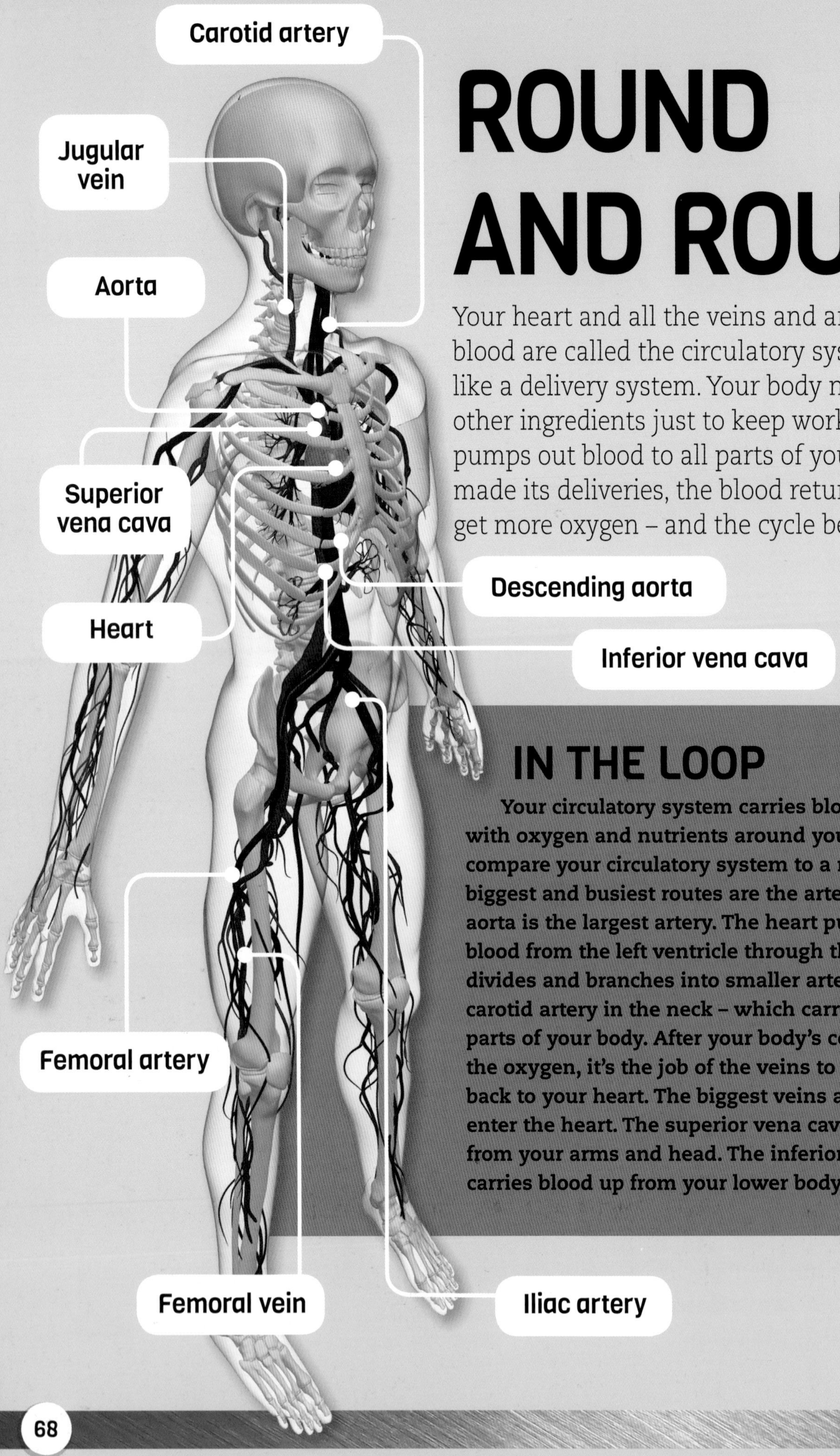

Labels (left side of diagram)

- Carotid artery
- Jugular vein
- Aorta
- Superior vena cava
- Heart
- Descending aorta
- Inferior vena cava
- Femoral artery
- Femoral vein
- Iliac artery

ROUND AND ROUND

Your heart and all the veins and arteries carrying blood are called the circulatory system. It works a lot like a delivery system. Your body needs oxygen and other ingredients just to keep working. So, your heart pumps out blood to all parts of your body. When it has made its deliveries, the blood returns to the heart to get more oxygen – and the cycle begins all over again.

IN THE LOOP

Your circulatory system carries blood loaded with oxygen and nutrients around your body. If you compare your circulatory system to a road network, the biggest and busiest routes are the arteries and veins. The aorta is the largest artery. The heart pumps oxygen-rich blood from the left ventricle through the aorta. The aorta divides and branches into smaller arteries – such as the carotid artery in the neck – which carry the blood to all parts of your body. After your body's cells have received the oxygen, it's the job of the veins to take your blood back to your heart. The biggest veins are the two that enter the heart. The superior vena cava carries blood from your arms and head. The inferior vena cava carries blood up from your lower body.

BRANCH LINES

Arteries and veins are connected by tiny tubes called capillaries. These are so thin that blood from the arteries passes through them easily. The blood cells release their oxygen to the surrounding body cells through the capillary wall. At the same time, they pick up waste from the body cells. The main type of waste is a gas called carbon dioxide. Then the blood travels into the veins, ready for transport back to the heart.

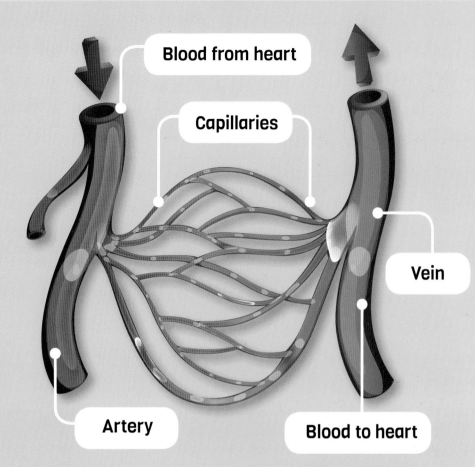

Blood from heart

Capillaries

Vein

Artery

Blood to heart

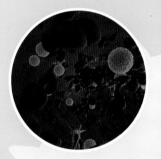

BLOOD CELLS

Your blood contains three main types of cell. Red blood cells collect oxygen from your lungs. This oxygen is packed into compartments inside the red blood cells, along with vitamins and other nutrients. White blood cells help your body to fight infection. Platelets are the smallest cells. Their job is to repair holes in the linings of blood vessels. They also help you to make a scab when you cut yourself. All the cells float inside a liquid called plasma.

The human body has about

100,000 km (60,000 miles)

of blood vessels – enough to go around the world about two and a half times!

TAKE CARE OF YOUR HEART

Your heart needs to be exercised regularly to stay healthy. It's not too hard to give it a gentle workout – after all, it beats more than 100,000 times every day and you don't need to do anything to make it work. Your body automatically produces a burst of electricity that triggers each of those heart beats.

HEALTHY HEART, HEALTHY YOU

Your heart may work automatically, but to keep a healthy heart, it's mostly up to you to make sure you don't make it struggle. For example, your heart is just the right size to pump your blood around your body. But if you put on too much weight, your heart can find the job much harder to do.

TAKE SOME EXERCISE

Regular exercise helps your heart stay healthy, and it keeps you fit. It also makes your heart stronger – it is a muscle, after all. If your heart has to struggle to pump blood around your body, then your muscles and other parts of your body, won't get enough oxygen. That means you'll have less energy, which is why people who are unfit get tired and out of breath very quickly.

Regular exercise helps strengthen your heart and improves circulation!

SMOKE SIGNALS

Smoking damages blood cells and causes a waxy substance to build up in the arteries. Over time, this substance hardens and makes it difficult for the blood to pass through the arteries. This can lead to heart disease, heart attacks, and even heart failure.

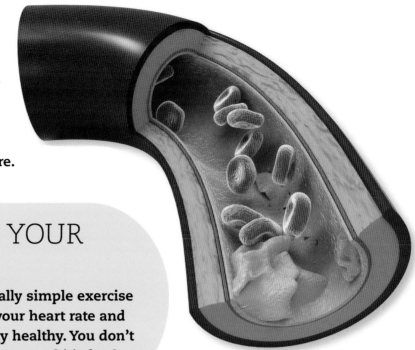

RUN FOR YOUR LIFE

Running is a really simple exercise that increases your heart rate and helps you to stay healthy. You don't need any equipment and it's free!

EAT HEART-HEALTHY FOOD

Eating fresh vegetables and fruit in a balanced diet is good for you, as you body gets the nutrients it needs to operate smoothly. Also, fresh foods don't contain added ingredients that can cause trouble with your heart and blood vessels.

 ACTIVITY

You can demonstrate the strain blockages create for blood vessels. Stretch a long balloon and cut the closed tip. Slide one end over a garden hose, hold it, and slowly turn the hose on. Water will come out of the other end just like a blood flow. Now pinch the far end. Water strains against the balloon just like blood that's been blocked.

SALTY SNACKS – GO EASY!

Too much salt can be bad for you. Eating too many salty snacks causes your body to hold on to more water. The extra liquid in your blood puts more pressure on the walls of the blood vessels and also on your heart.

A BREATH OF FRESH AIR

Your lungs make up one of the largest organs in your body. They work with your respiratory (breathing) system to allow you to take in fresh air. Although you can't see it, the air you breathe is made up of several gases. Oxygen is the most important gas because your body needs it for energy and growth.

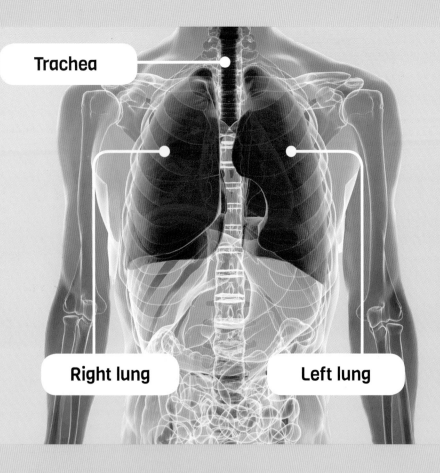

Trachea

Right lung

Left lung

A TRIP DOWN THE TRACHEA

As you breathe in, air travels from your mouth and nose down to your lungs. Both of your lungs do the same job, but your left lung is slightly smaller, to leave space for your heart. The air travels down your windpipe, called the trachea. The trachea is lined with tiny hairs called cilia which catch dust particles that may have floated in with the air.

BRANCHING OFF

When your trachea reaches your lungs, it divides into two tubes, called bronchi, which connect to the lungs. Here, they branch into smaller bronchi, which fork again into even smaller tubes, about the width of a human hair, called bronchioles. There are around 30,000 bronchioles in each of your lungs. They end in tiny air sacs, called alveoli. A single alveoli is called an alveolus.

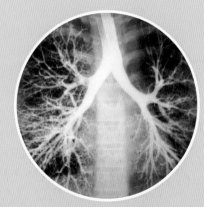

GAS EXCHANGE

The job of your respiratory system is to bring oxygen gas into your body and get rid of the waste, which is another gas called carbon dioxide. As you breathe in, oxygen passes through the walls of the alveoli into the blood cells in the capillaries. Once it's loaded with oxygen, the blood is ready to move on. But before it does, the blood cells release the waste carbon dioxide into the alveoli. Then, the process is reversed so that you breathe out the waste.

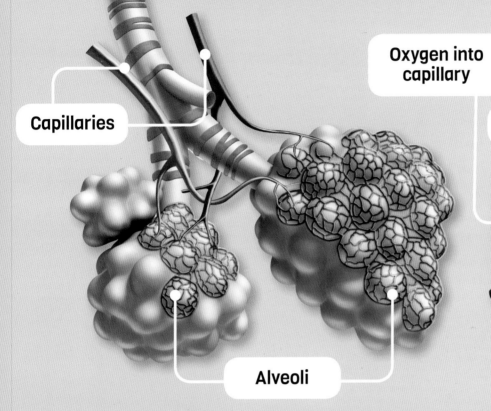

Bronchiole

Capillaries

Oxygen into capillary

Carbon dioxide into alveolus

Capillary

Alveolus

Oxygen in

Alveoli

Waste products out

STRAIGHT TO THE HEART

From the lungs, oxygen-rich blood heads straight to the heart through the pulmonary vein, ready to be pumped around the body. The movement of blood between the heart and the lungs is called pulmonary circulation.

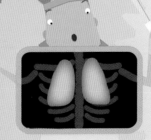

If you spread out the 300 million alveoli in a pair of adult lungs, their surface area would be about as large as a tennis court!

SPEAK OUT!

One of the hardest-working muscles in your body is your diaphragm. It makes sure you breathe in air that's rich in oxygen, and breathe out air that's full of waste. That flow of air that comes out of you also creates the sounds you make to communicate – whether it's a hushed whisper, a loud shout, or a happy song!

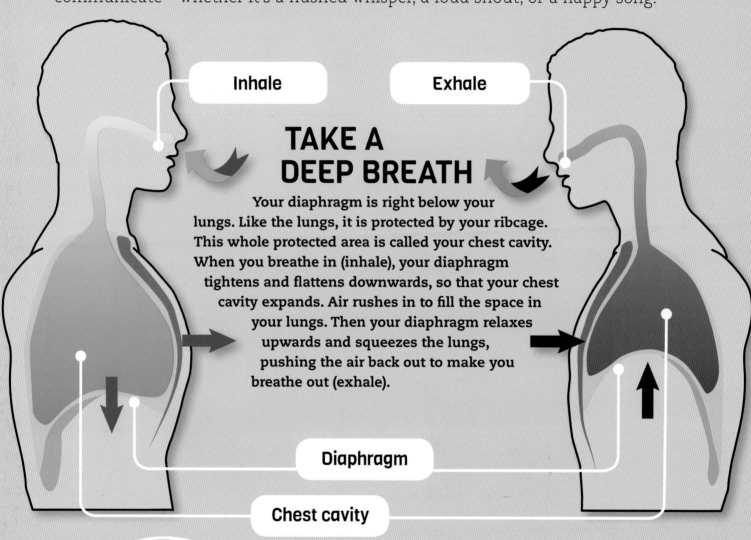

Inhale

Exhale

TAKE A DEEP BREATH

Your diaphragm is right below your lungs. Like the lungs, it is protected by your ribcage. This whole protected area is called your chest cavity. When you breathe in (inhale), your diaphragm tightens and flattens downwards, so that your chest cavity expands. Air rushes in to fill the space in your lungs. Then your diaphragm relaxes upwards and squeezes the lungs, pushing the air back out to make you breathe out (exhale).

Diaphragm

Chest cavity

OUT IT GOES

Breathing out is just as important as breathing in! Your body needs to get rid of carbon dioxide and other waste. If carbon dioxide builds up in your blood or lungs, it can affect your muscles and your breathing. You can hold your breath for a short time, but eventually your body forces you to breathe out!

SOMETHING TO SHOUT ABOUT

The sounds you make are created in the larynx, or voicebox, which sits at the top of your trachea (windpipe). When you talk, your vocal cords in your voice box tighten up and move closer together. Air from the lungs is forced between them and this makes them move, or vibrate. This vibration produces the sound of your voice. Your tongue, lips, and teeth help you to form this sound into words. As you grow older, your larynx gets bigger and this makes your voice deepen.

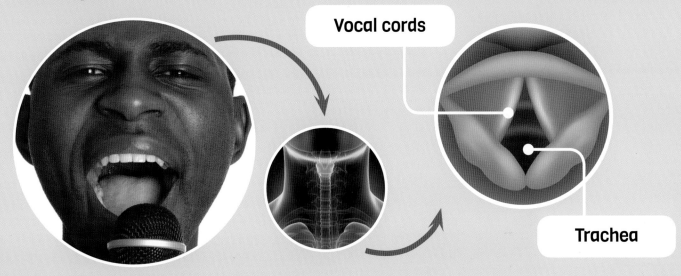

Vocal cords

Trachea

ACTIVITY

Yawning is contagious! Sit down with a friend and then both try and relax. Then, ask your friend to yawn. You'll soon find yourself joining in as well! A yawn is an exercise for your lungs because it stretches them and keeps them fit.

In 1994, Annalisa Flanagan won a shouting contest and broke the world record for the loudest voice by shouting the word "quiet!"

DID YOU KNOW?

Your heart and lungs, along with their major systems (circulatory and respiratory) are amazing. Here are some facts about the organs you rely on to stay alive, healthy, and active!

WORKING 24/7

You may go to sleep at night, but your body keeps on working. Your body needs nutrients and oxygen all of the time to keep your circulatory, respiratory, and other systems working 24/7. So, even while you're at rest, your heart keeps pumping blood around your body and your heart keeps breathing to keep you going.

The average person takes around 16 breaths a minute, or 960 breaths an hour, or 23,040 breaths a day, or 8,409,600 breaths a year, or more than 670 million breaths in a lifetime.

After all the work it's been doing overnight, your body needs to recharge its batteries. That's why breakfast is such an important meal. It boosts your energy levels and keeps you going until lunchtime.

BLOOD AT WORK

Your blood is full of metal. The iron-rich protein haemoglobin is the substance in blood that actually carries oxygen. When it reaches your muscles, the haemoglobin releases the oxygen. At the same time, it collects waste carbon dioxide and takes it away. The picture on the right shows a computer-generated model of a haemoglobin molecule.

SELF DESTRUCT!

Body cells such as red blood cells don't live forever. They die either because they have become infected, or because they self-destruct. Once they stop working as well as they should, cells are programmed to release chemicals to break themselves apart. The bits pass out of your body as waste.

GIVING BLOOD

Healthy people can give blood to help others in need. If you give blood you should not exercise for a few hours afterward. That's because your body needs time to build up fresh blood to replace the blood that's been taken away. Exercise would call for extra oxygen too soon. Although everyone's blood does the same job, there are four different types of blood, called "groups".

THIN AIR

Up in the mountains, the air becomes "thinner". That means there is less of it and it is harder to breath. For a climber on a high mountain, each breath gives the body less oxygen than it would lower down at sea level. In response, the climber's body gradually makes more red blood cells to do a better job of capturing the available oxygen.

TESTING YOUR LIMITS

Your body is well-equipped to keep your muscles supplied with oxygen. When you exercise hard, your circulatory and respiratory systems start working really hard. Their job is to get oxygen to your muscles as fast as possible and to get rid of carbon dioxide and other waste quickly.

PUMP IT UP

All types of exercise call on you to be fit. Training regularly makes you fitter so you can exercise for longer. That's because using muscles often, and increasing their workload, makes them stronger. This is the basis of all training, and it works for your heart just as much as for your leg or arm muscles. When you exercise, you need to breathe harder and your heart needs to pump faster, but all that extra oxygen gets used more efficiently.

A New Zealand couple in their 60s set a world record by running a marathon (42km / 26.2 miles) every day in 2013. They finished with marathon number 366 on New Year's Day 2014!

ACTIVITY

Ask a friend to take your pulse rate (see page 66) and write it down. Then, jog up and down a flight of stairs three times and ask your friend to take your pulse again. You'll see that your heart has begun to work harder to get blood to your muscles.

TRAIN HIGH, RUN LOW

Athletes often get fitter by "training high and running low". They spend weeks training at high altitudes where the air is thinner (see page 77). Here, their bodies produce more red blood cells to capture the oxygen in the air more efficiently. Then, when they compete at lower altitudes, each breath brings in more oxygen. More oxygen plus more red blood cells means more energy – and maybe the difference between first and second place!

FEEL THE BURN

People talk about "feeling the burn" when they exercise hard. The "burn" comes from lactic acid, which is produced as muscles use up all of the available oxygen from the blood. Hold an orange in one hand, with your arm outstretched, for a minute... or as long as you can. After a while, can you "feel the burn"? This painful sensation is your body's way of telling you to stop whatever you are doing!

EAT, RELAX

After you've eaten a meal, your digestive system needs a lot of blood. That's why you shouldn't exercise after you've eaten. Your body finds it hard to digest food and exercise at the same time. As you exercise, your body concentrates on the muscles that are working hardest. It isn't just your heart and lungs that get to work. Your nervous system helps slow the flow of blood to other organs that don't need it urgently. It does that by narrowing the blood vessels leading there, just like squeezing shut a garden hose. At the same time, it widens the blood vessels leading to the active muscles.

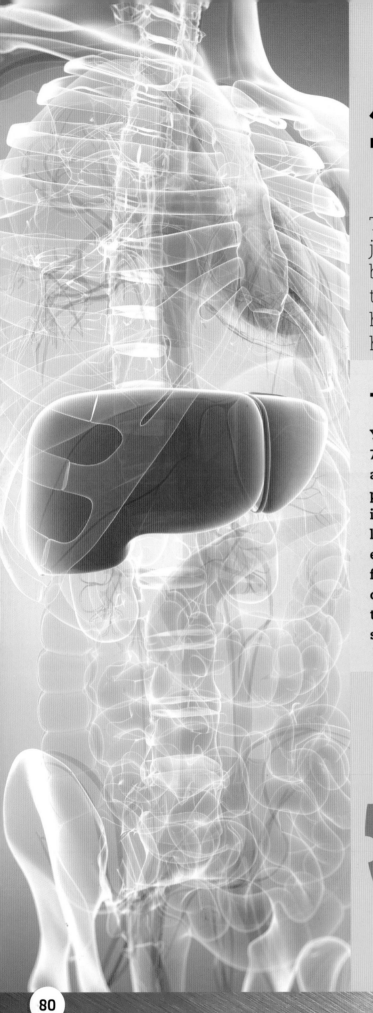

JACK OF ALL TRADES

The liver is your body's largest organ with many jobs to do. It produces proteins that give your blood the power to heal you. It filters and cleans the blood in your circulatory system. And it also helps you get the goodness out of foods that are hard to digest, such as fats.

THE BODY'S FACTORY

Your liver sits just below your diaphragm (see page 74), on your right side. Like your diaphragm, lungs, and heart, it's protected by your ribcage. Although it's part of your digestive system (see page 36), your liver is vital to your blood and circulatory system too. It's like a factory with different departments. Some make essential substances. Others separate useful nutrients from waste in the blood. All that work uses up lots of energy. That's why there's a major vessel called the hepatic artery bringing oxygen-rich blood straight from your heart to your liver.

The liver is the only internal organ that can regenerate itself if it gets damaged. It also holds about 1/7 of your body's total blood supply at any given time!

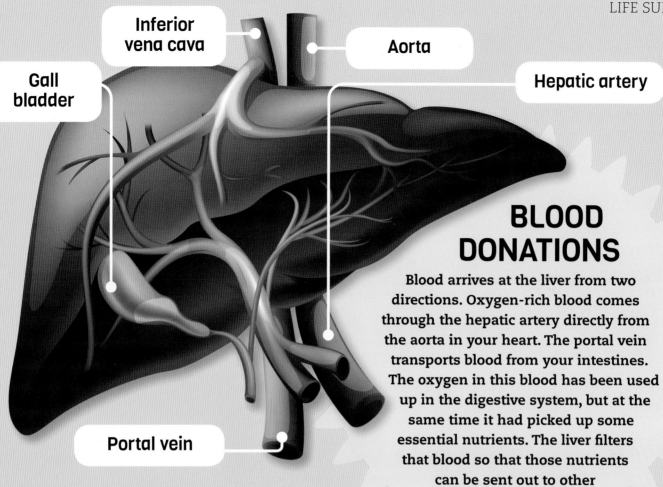

Inferior vena cava

Aorta

Gall bladder

Hepatic artery

Portal vein

BLOOD DONATIONS

Blood arrives at the liver from two directions. Oxygen-rich blood comes through the hepatic artery directly from the aorta in your heart. The portal vein transports blood from your intestines. The oxygen in this blood has been used up in the digestive system, but at the same time it had picked up some essential nutrients. The liver filters that blood so that those nutrients can be sent out to other parts of the body.

WASTE MANAGEMENT

Your liver is made up of thousands of small features called lobules (pictured). Each lobule is connected to many vessels carrying blood to and from the liver. The lobules filter your blood. Useful nutrients are broken down and then sent back into the blood. The liver uses some of the filtered waste material to create bile, the substance that helps you digest fats (see page 36). Other wastes get sent in the blood to the kidneys (see page 38), which gets rid of them in your urine.

HEALING POWERS

When you cut or graze yourself, your liver helps your body to patch itself up. When your skin is damaged, special blood cells, called platelets, get to work to stop the bleeding and to create a patch – or scab – to keep germs out (as in this picture). The platelets need to combine with certain proteins called clotting factors. Clotting is a medical word to describe what happens as blood turns into a solid. These proteins are produced in your liver.

GET THE MESSAGE?

Hypothalamus

Your body sends messages to itself all the time. These chemical messages are called hormones. Some hormones produce changes over a long period, for example telling your body how to grow. Others can help you deal with sudden problems, like being chased by a vicious dog.

Thyroid gland

CHEMICAL MESSENGERS

Glands are organs in your body that produce certain types of chemicals. These chemicals have different effects in your body. Glands send off chemical hormones into your blood, so that they can reach the necessary bits of your body. Some hormones tell other organs how active they need to be – to help you digest food. Hormones also help you to deal with emergencies, giving you extra strength. Some hormones even go to other glands, to get them to make more hormones!

Thymus gland

Adrenal glands

Reproductive glands

Epinephrine is called the "fight or flight" hormone. Your body makes it when you're in a situation where you might have to fight, or run away quickly!

CHECK YOUR SPEED

The thyroid gland, in the front of your neck (shown here in pink), sends out a hormone to control how fast the cells in your body are using up nutrients to produce energy. That speed is called your metabolic rate. People with a high metabolic rate burn energy more quickly than those with a slower metabolic rate. The thyroid gland wraps around the front of your larynx (shown here in white). You can feel it under the skin in the front of your neck.

FEELING SLEEPY?

The pineal gland is found in your brain and is shaped like a small pine cone, which is how it got its name. This gland makes a hormone called melatonin, which regulates your sleep patterns. So when you're feeling sleepy and ready for bed, it's the pineal gland that's responsible.

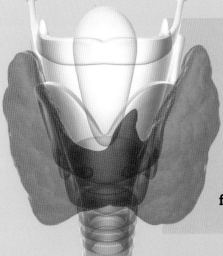

LISTEN TO YOUR MASTER

Although only about the size of a pea, the pituitary gland – located at the base of your brain – is often called the "master gland". That's because it sends out hormones to check on other glands, making sure they work in balance with each other. Being so close to the brain helps – the pituitary gland reacts almost instantly to signals sent out by the brain.

TAKING
CONTROL

Just like the conductor of an orchestra, your brain is making decisions and guiding you all the time. Different areas of your brain concentrate on special jobs. Some of those jobs need quick action – like telling your body which muscles to use when you're running or swimming. Others, like doing your homework, take more time.

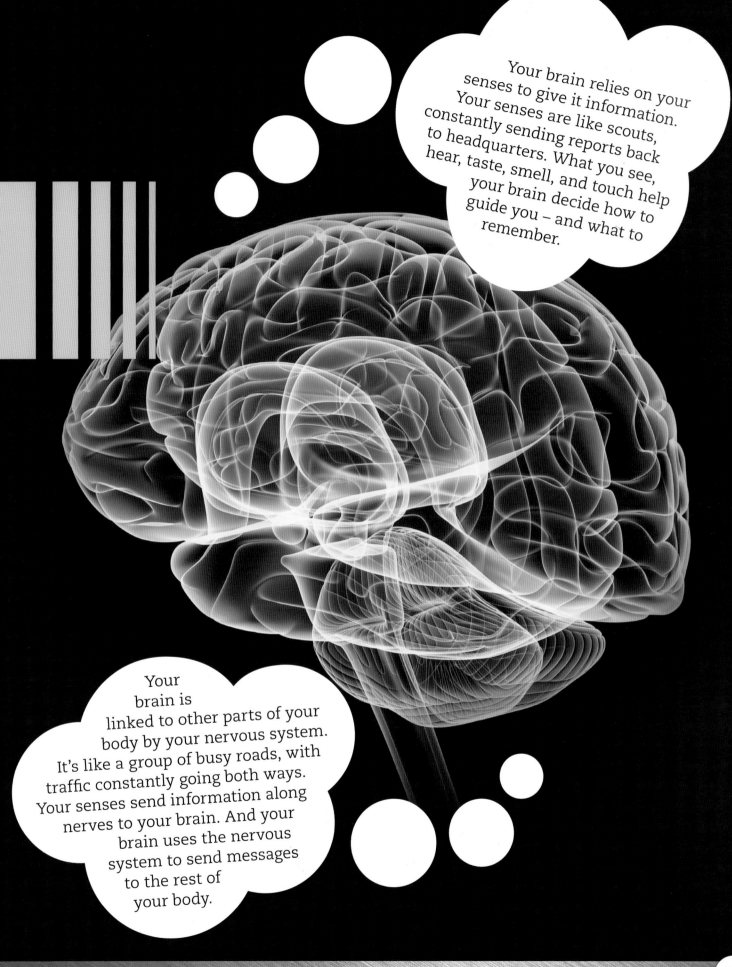

Your brain relies on your senses to give it information. Your senses are like scouts, constantly sending reports back to headquarters. What you see, hear, taste, smell, and touch help your brain decide how to guide you – and what to remember.

Your brain is linked to other parts of your body by your nervous system. It's like a group of busy roads, with traffic constantly going both ways. Your senses send information along nerves to your brain. And your brain uses the nervous system to send messages to the rest of your body.

THE BRAIN IS BOSS

Brain stem

Cerebrum

Your brain is the boss of your body. It is constantly checking new information, storing the things you learn and the experiences you have, and sending orders out to your body, telling it what to do.

YOUR HARD DRIVE

Your brain weighs around 1.5 kg (3 pounds) and looks a lot like a wrinkled grapefruit. Inside it are about 100 billion nerve cells, the headquarters of your nervous system. The human brain is often compared to a computer. It sends and receives signals to the rest of your body through the spinal cord, which extends down from it. Each part of your brain is responsible for a special job. It could be deciding whether you feel angry, which muscles to use, or whether to put on a warmer coat.

Spinal cord

Cerebellum

SORRY – WRONG DEPARTMENT

Different parts of your brain concentrate on different jobs. The largest part is the cerebrum, which is the bit you'd see if you took the top of your head off. This is where your thinking gets done and where you store your memories. The cerebellum, at the back of your brain, controls all your movements. Your brain stem connects your brain with your spinal cord, and it looks after activities such as digestion, blood flow, and breathing.

AUTO PILOT

At first, some things such as riding a bike or learning a dance routine, need concentration and practice. But after a while, your cerebellum takes over and remembers how to do these things, so you can do them automatically "without thinking".

LEFT OR RIGHT?

Your cerebrum has two halves – left and right. The left half seems to be linked to "practical" actions such as mathematics and speech. The right half concentrates on more "artistic" things such as music and recognizing faces. You use both halves, but right-handed people seem to use their left half more... and left-handers seem to use their right half more!

ACTIVITY

Put a dozen different objects on a tray. Ask your friends to look at the objects for one minute. Then, remove the tray. Now, ask your friends to write down as many of the objects as they are able to remember. Which one of your friends is the best at this kind of mental task?

Your brain operates on the same amount of power used by a 10-watt light bulb!

WHAT A NERVE!

Your brain and spinal cord are linked to a huge network of nerves. These carry information all around your body. Together, they make up your nervous system. In just a fraction of a second, messages are sent back and forth from your brain, deciding all that you do and think.

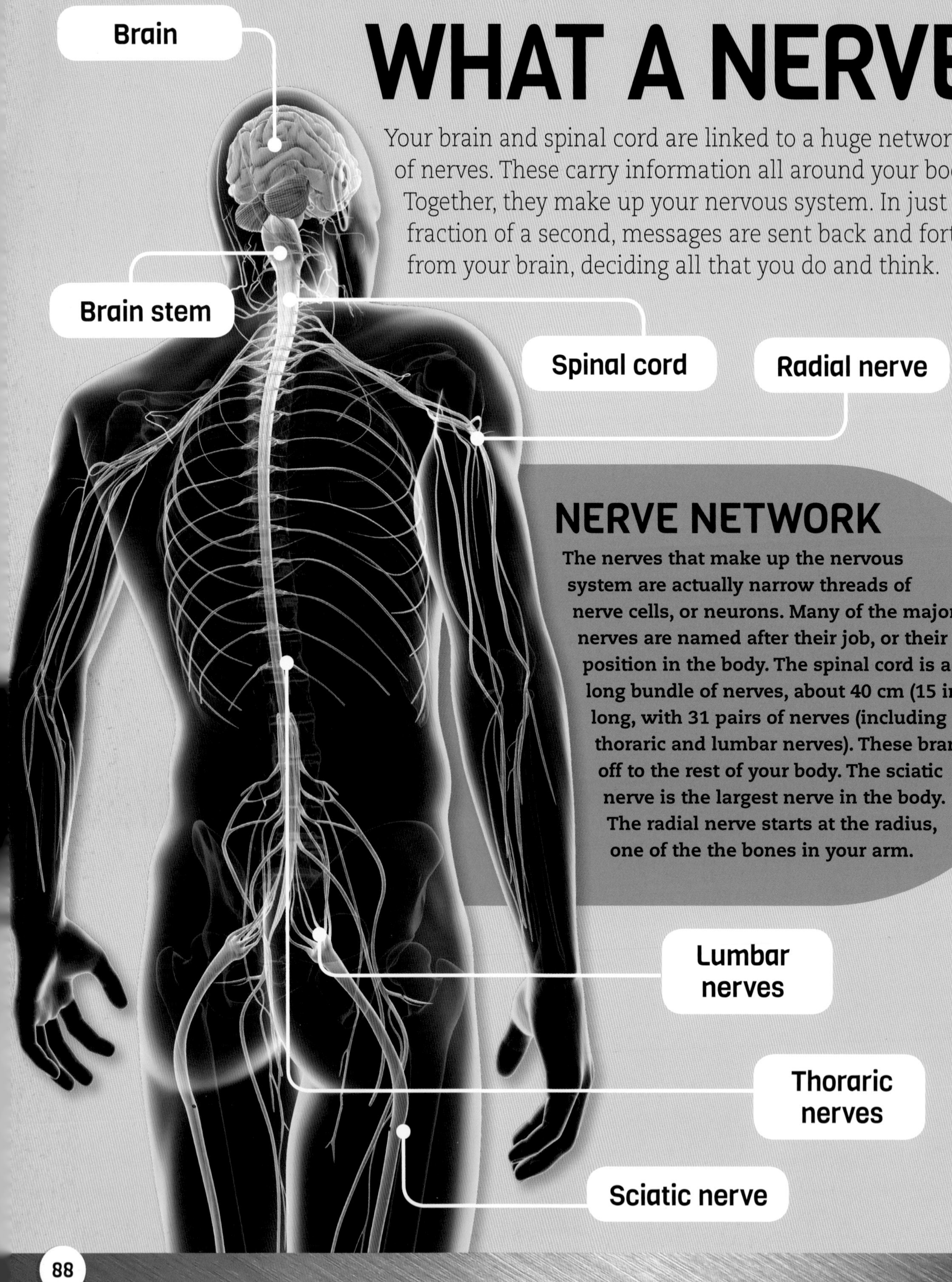

Brain

Brain stem

Spinal cord

Radial nerve

NERVE NETWORK

The nerves that make up the nervous system are actually narrow threads of nerve cells, or neurons. Many of the major nerves are named after their job, or their position in the body. The spinal cord is a long bundle of nerves, about 40 cm (15 in) long, with 31 pairs of nerves (including the thoraric and lumbar nerves). These branch off to the rest of your body. The sciatic nerve is the largest nerve in the body. The radial nerve starts at the radius, one of the the bones in your arm.

Lumbar nerves

Thoraric nerves

Sciatic nerve

TO AND FRO

Nerves take information to and from the brain. Sensory neurons send messages from the body to the brain. Motor neurons carry messages from the brain to the muscles to tell them when and how to move. Other neurons send information between the sensory and motor neurons.

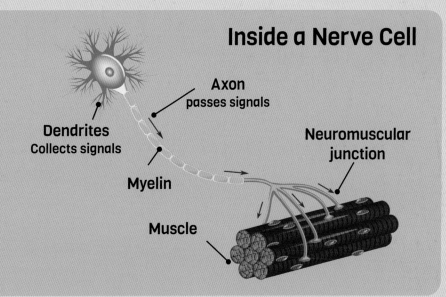

Inside a Nerve Cell

Axon
passes signals

Dendrites
Collects signals

Neuromuscular junction

Myelin

Muscle

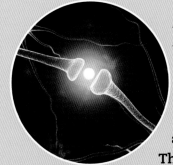

HOW SHOCKING

Neurons pick up and send signals as electrical pulses. The electric signal creates a chemical change at the synapse – the place where two neurons join together. This allows the electrical pulse to jump across the gap. The pulse continues along like this, neuron by neuron, as it passes all along the nerve – and this all happens in less than a second!

Crossing your arms can reduce pain in your hands or arms. The "pain message" is disrupted as it travels through the nerve cells!

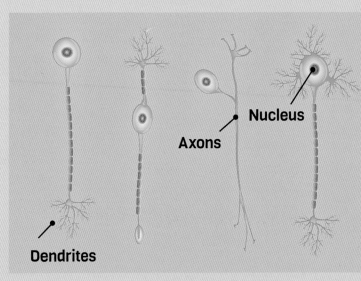

Nucleus

Axons

Dendrites

CHAIN REACTION

Neurons come in many different shapes, but they all have a nucleus and special parts called dendrites and axons. Dendrites picks up signals from other neurons and axons pass them on. Neurons are lined up in long chains, but they don't actually touch. Messages travel from neuron to neuron as the signals jump across small gaps, or synapses, between them.

EYE SPY

Think of how much information you get from your eyes – playing games, watching films, or reading this page. Your eyes constantly receive images, focus them, and then send signals to your brain. They tell you what's around you, how close or big things are, whether they're moving, and much more.

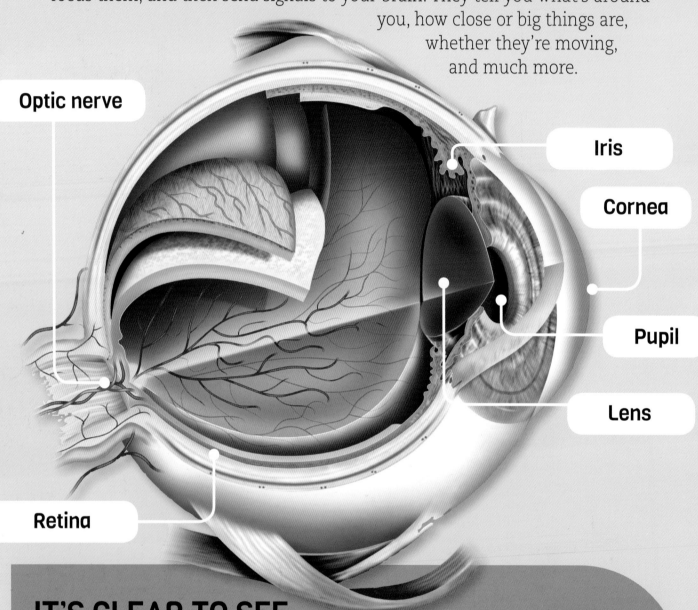

Optic nerve

Iris

Cornea

Pupil

Lens

Retina

IT'S CLEAR TO SEE

Whenever you look at an object, the light from it enters your eye through your pupil, the dark opening in the middle of your eye. The iris then changes the size of the pupil, depending on how bright the light is. The lens focuses the light onto the retina at the back of your eye. Here, the light is turned into an electrical burst which travels along the optic nerve to the brain, where an image of what you are seeing is formed.

TWO EYES ARE BETTER THAN ONE

Why do you have two eyes? It's to help you judge how far away things are. When you look at something, your two eyes see the image slightly differently. The difference depends on how far way an object is. Your brain receives both images and instantly works out the distance to the object. This ability is called depth perception.

3D WORLD TURNED UPSIDE-DOWN

Your retina contains millions of special receptor cells, as shown on the left. They respond to light entering your eye. By focusing images on your retina, your lens turns them upside-down. So, in order for you to see properly, your brain has to turn them the right way up again. Your brain also needs to merge the two slightly different images captured by each of your eyes into one. By doing so, your brain creates a 3D picture of the thing you are looking at.

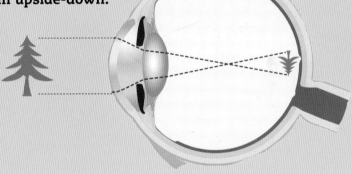

ACTIVITY

Hold a pencil in each hand and straighten your arms in front of you. Close one eye and try to touch the tip of one pencil to the other. Now try it with both your eyes open. It should be a lot easier, thanks to your depth perception.

The size of your eyes barely changes from the day you're born to when you become an adult.

HEAR, HEAR!

What you hear as sounds starts out as waves in the air. Your ears pick up those sound waves and change them into signals that are sent to your brain. Your brain makes sense of the patterns in the sounds you hear, so you recognize them as music, speech, or familiar voices. Other sounds, like screams or sirens, warn you of danger.

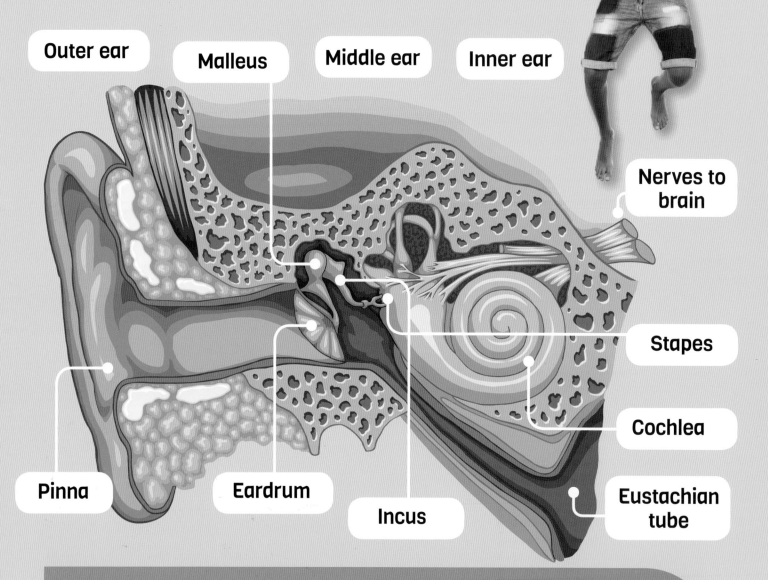

Outer ear

Malleus

Middle ear

Inner ear

Nerves to brain

Stapes

Cochlea

Eustachian tube

Incus

Eardrum

Pinna

SOUND WAVES

The pinna is the part of your outer ear that you can see. Its job is to capture sounds so that they travel down the ear canal into your middle ear. Those sound waves are turned into movements, or vibrations, in your middle ear, which are passed to your inner ear.

THE DRUM SECTION

Your eardrum is where your outer ear meets your middle ear. Sound waves make it move, or vibrate. The vibrations cause three tiny bones – the malleus, incus, and stapes – to vibrate. And those vibrations create waves in liquid inside the cochlea of the inner ear. Tiny hairs on the cochlea then pick up that movement and send signals to the nerve cells. That's where the nervous system takes over and sends the signals to the brain. And that's how you "hear" sounds.

Ears make earwax to clean and protect the ear. Tiny hairs, called cilia, move the wax forward out of the ear!

FEELING THE PRESSURE

You sometimes get a popping feeling in your ears going along a mountain road or on a plane. This is because the air inside your ears is at a different pressure from the air outside your ears. As air pressure increases on the outside, it pushes in on the eardrum. To balance this out, your body takes in air through the Eustachian tubes, which connect your ears to your throat. Your ears then "pop" as the air is balanced, or equalized, on both sides of the eardrum.

WHAT'S THE FREQUENCY?

Sounds and hearing are all about vibrations. How fast or slow the sound waves are moving decides whether you hear them as high or low sounds. That speed is called the frequency – because it describes how frequently the air is vibrating. Some frequencies are too high or low for humans to hear. If you blow a dog whistle, your pet will hear it even though you can't. You lose your ability to hear some very high or very low frequencies as you get older. In fact, some phones have ring tones that grown-ups can't hear!

SMELLS GOOD, TASTES GREAT

TASTY!

The picture above shows the bumps on your tongue in close-up, called taste buds. Taste buds have special cells that pick up particular chemicals (tastes) in the food you eat. Sweet taste cells respond when you're eating chocolate or cake. Salty cells pick up signals when you're eating fries or corn chips.

For a long time, scientists thought we could pick out four main tastes – sweet, sour, salty, and bitter. They now accept there's a fifth taste, called umami, which comes out strongly in meat. And they suggest that maybe you can detect six or even more tastes. You might be able to taste the calcium in vegetables, or the carbon dioxide in a can of cola.

Stick out your tongue and look at it in a mirror. You'll see lots of pink bumps. That's where your body tastes food. Special cells pick out certain tastes and send messages to your brain. Most of those cells are on your tongue, but you also have some taste cells on the roof of your mouth and the back of your throat. Meanwhile your nose helps you get a fuller picture of what you're tasting.

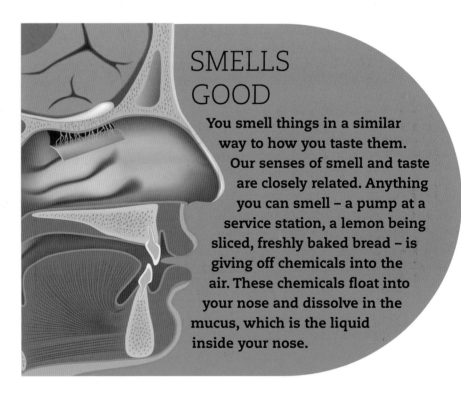

SMELLS GOOD

You smell things in a similar way to how you taste them. Our senses of smell and taste are closely related. Anything you can smell – a pump at a service station, a lemon being sliced, freshly baked bread – is giving off chemicals into the air. These chemicals float into your nose and dissolve in the mucus, which is the liquid inside your nose.

SMELL SIGNALS

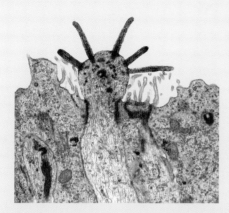

Special cells called chemoreceptors (shown here on the left) are found deep inside your nose. These react to particular dissolved chemicals. They send a signal further into your nose, and that signal then travels along nerves to different parts of your brain. Smell is an important sense. For example, if we smell smoke or gas, it can alert us to danger.

Your nose also helps you to taste things. As you chew, your food gives off chemicals. Some of them float up into your nose, which "smells" them as normal. You need this smell as much as you do the taste signals from your mouth in order to get the full picture of how your food tastes.

Tastes and smells can trigger memories that stay with you for life.

Our bodies produce certain chemicals when we're afraid, so other people might be able to "smell fear".

Your nose plays an important part in tasting. That's why you can't taste food with a bad cold!

HOW TOUCHING

Your sense of touch is important. Without it, you wouldn't know that the stovetop was dangerously hot, or that the thorns on a plant were sharp enough to cut you – or even how pleasant the spring sunshine feels on your bare arm.

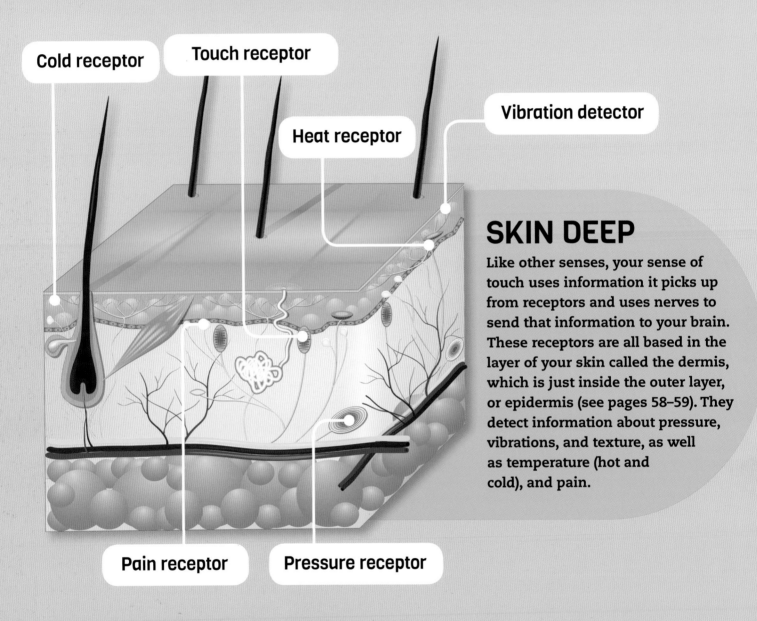

Cold receptor

Touch receptor

Heat receptor

Vibration detector

Pain receptor

Pressure receptor

SKIN DEEP

Like other senses, your sense of touch uses information it picks up from receptors and uses nerves to send that information to your brain. These receptors are all based in the layer of your skin called the dermis, which is just inside the outer layer, or epidermis (see pages 58–59). They detect information about pressure, vibrations, and texture, as well as temperature (hot and cold), and pain.

TAKE THE HEAT OFF

Signals about heat go to and from the brain in a flash. You could be badly burned if you didn't react quickly to heat. It takes only about 15 milliseconds (thousandths of a second) for the information to reach your brain... and a similar time on the way back. That's usually enough time to get you to pull your hand away from a hot stove or kettle.

TOO COLD!

Cold receptors in your fingertips pick up information when you touch an ice cube. That sensation of cold then becomes an electrical signal that's sent along the nerves to your spinal cord, and travels directly to your brain. Your brain quickly responds to this information and sends instructions back to the motor neurons that control the muscles in your fingertips: "too cold – stop touching it".

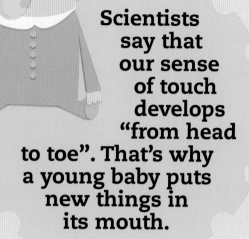

Scientists say that our sense of touch develops "from head to toe". That's why a young baby puts new things in its mouth.

SENSITIVE BODY PARTS

This strange man (on the right) is actually a sensory body map. He shows what the body would look like if each part grew in proportion to the number of sensory neurons it contained. The hands, lips, and mouth are all huge because they are packed with sensory nerves. However, the arms, body and legs are small and skinny because they have fewer sensory receptors.

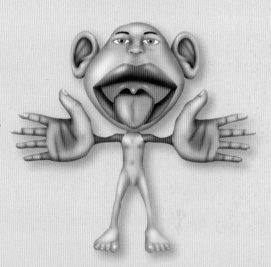

WHAT A PAIN

Imagine what would happen if you started to step on a nail or twisted your ankle and it didn't hurt. You could injure yourself more seriously if you didn't know about it straight away. That's why your body has special receptors that tell you when something hurts. Your body has more than 3 million pain receptors. Apart from causing a sharp pain to cause you to move away from danger, they also produce a duller pain if you have an injury. The pain stops you from using that part of your body until it heals.

CHANGING YOUR MIND

Human beings are very good at adapting to situations both mentally and physically. You could probably learn to write with your other hand if you broke your arm. Athletes at the Paralympics show the whole world how they can overcome disabilities to take part in their sport. It's all down to finding ways to get the most out of your body, your brain, your senses, and your nervous system.

Some blind people can "see" where they're going by making clicking sounds and listening to the echo to judge distances to objects. It's the same method that bats use!

A visually impaired skier has to rely on his sense of hearing to race down the mountain. He listens to his guide, and the other sounds he can hear around him.

BRAIN REWIRING

People with poor vision can wear glasses or contact lenses to correct their sight. Hearing aids can help people to hear more clearly. But a person who is completely blind or deaf often uses their other senses to help replace the "missing" sense. Blind people use their sense of touch to read by running their fingertips across raised dots on the surface of Braille pages. Deaf people learn to communicate by lip-reading and sign language. Scientists believe that the brain "rewires" itself to use the areas that would otherwise have been devoted to the missing sense.

WHAT ARE YOUR STRENGTHS?

Your brain may be flexible and good at adapting to changing situations, but it still has its strengths and weaknesses. In fact, different areas of your brain do different kinds of work and individual people have varying strengths and skills. You may be excellent with numbers if your frontal lobe is particularly active, or you may prefer arts and languages if your parietal lobe is more developed. You might be great at complicated multiplication problems. Someone else may play the piano brilliantly. Scientists agree that some parts of your brain work better than others.

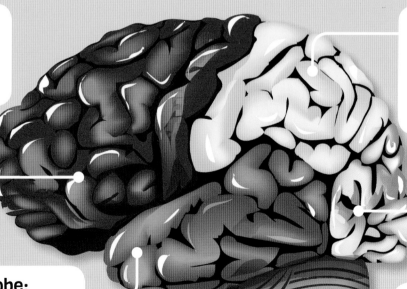

Frontal lobe: reasoning, planning, movement, emotions, problem-solving

Parietal lobe: language, touch, pressure, temperature, pain

Occipital lobe: sight

Temporal lobe: hearing, taste, sound, memory

Cerebellum

Spinal cord

BEHIND THE SCENES

Your body has a whole system of automatic-pilot functions that keeps it ticking over. The autonomic nervous system is the central command of this system. Without you being aware of it, this network of nerves controls your breathing, heart rate, swallowing, digestion, blinking, production of saliva, how much you sweat, and whether you need to urinate.

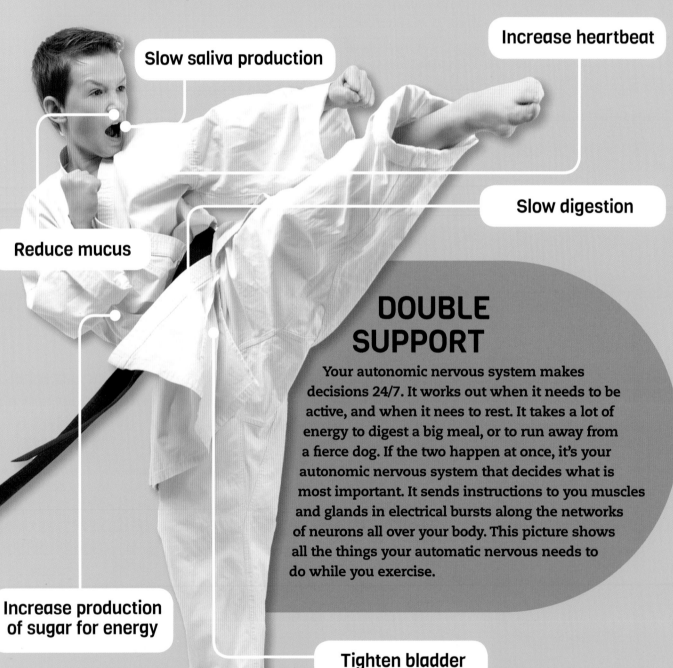

Slow saliva production

Increase heartbeat

Slow digestion

Reduce mucus

DOUBLE SUPPORT

Your autonomic nervous system makes decisions 24/7. It works out when it needs to be active, and when it nees to rest. It takes a lot of energy to digest a big meal, or to run away from a fierce dog. If the two happen at once, it's your autonomic nervous system that decides what is most important. It sends instructions to you muscles and glands in electrical bursts along the networks of neurons all over your body. This picture shows all the things your automatic nervous needs to do while you exercise.

Increase production of sugar for energy

Tighten bladder

Your eyes automatically blink around 12 times a minute. So in your lifetime, you will spend about 434 days in darkness due to blinking!

COILED FOR ACTION

The autonomic nervous system springs into action when you're faced with something scary or exciting. It sets up a "fight or flight" response (see page 82). This gets your heart and lungs to work harder so that you're more alert and have more energy.

REST AND DIGEST

When things are calmer, your digestive system needs oxygen-rich blood to get on with its job. That's when the autonomic nervous system changes the setting to "rest and digest". Your muscles need less blood, so your heart rate and breathing rate can slow down.

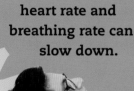

THE BRAIN IN YOUR GUT

A network of about 100 million neurons runs through the lining of your entire digestive system. It's a special part of the autonomic nervous system, known as the enteric nervous system. Although it has far fewer nerve cells than the brain in your head, scientists sometimes call it your second brain, or the "brain in the gut". It directs the way you digest food and also what to do if it detects something that could make you ill. So if you've ever thrown up after eating something that didn't agree with you, it's time to thank the brain in your gut!

TIME TO SLEEP

You know for sure that you need sleep to be alert the next day for schoolwork, to be able to think straight. But scientists now believe that sleep helps your body in many different, and often unexpected, ways. And sometimes the only way to work out what these are is to find out what happens when a person doesn't get enough sleep...

GET SOME SHUT-EYE

Sleep does more than simply allow your "batteries to recharge". Important changes take place in your brain – and in the rest of your body – as you sleep. For example, sleep affects production of the hormone that controls how you grow. So it seems that having enough sleep helps you to grow at a normal rate.

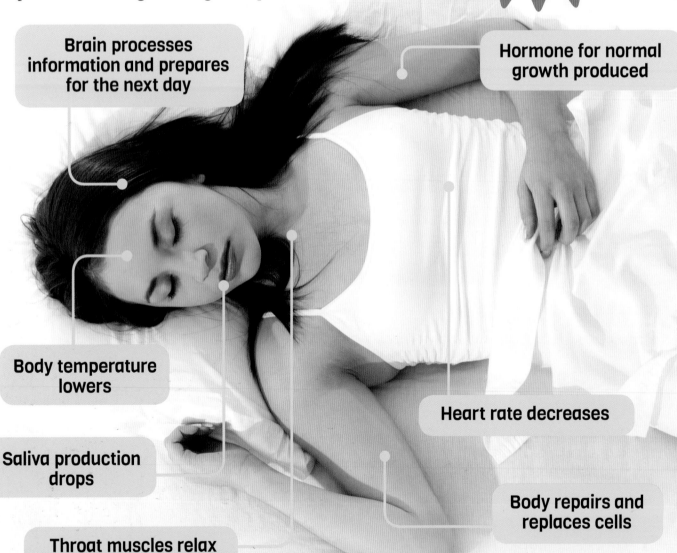

Brain processes information and prepares for the next day

Hormone for normal growth produced

Body temperature lowers

Heart rate decreases

Saliva production drops

Body repairs and replaces cells

Throat muscles relax

NOT ENOUGH SLEEP

Scientists know a lot about the benefits of sleep from studying people who don't sleep enough. Lack of sleep makes a person more likely to catch colds and other infections – so sleep has an effect on your immune system, which fights infection and keeps you healthy. People who go for several days without sleep usually become very confused. It seems that the right amount of sleep is vital to help your brain remain in control.

The French military commander Napoleon Bonaparte would go for days without sleep, but then would take a short nap just before a battle!

SWEET DREAMS

You only dream during the REM stage of your sleep cycle – but you get up to five of those each night. Beyond that, no one can say for sure exactly why or how you dream. People once thought that dreams could predict the future. Scientists no longer believe that, but some think that dreams help you sort out what's important to remember and what you can safely forget.

THE SLEEP CYCLE

You go through different stages when you sleep. These stages are known as the sleep cycle. A cycle lasts about 90 minutes, so when you've finished the REM stage, the cycle starts again.

Stage 1

You're half awake and half asleep – muscles begin to relax

Stage 2

In a light sleep, body temperature drops, breathing and heart rate slow down

Stages 3 and 4

In a deep sleep, breathing and heart rate at lowest levels, muscles relaxed, tissue growth and repair, hormones are released

Stage 5

Rapid Eye Movement (known as REM) occurs. Your eyes and other parts of your body become active. Although you're still asleep, your brain is active and dreams occur

YOUR PERSONAL COMPUTER?

Could a powerful computer do all your thinking just as well as your brain? The computer could certainly do lots of calculating, but it could never take over completely because it can't think or feel for itself. That's where your mind has the advantage. It's all about consciousness.

THINK FOR YOURSELF

Scientists have studied the brain for centuries, but many mysteries remain. They can see how electrical impulses travel from neuron to neuron, and how certain parts of the brain guide your movement, speech, language, and emotions. That much is like looking at a complicated computer, which also has elements to do special jobs. But you're more than a well-run machine. You can choose to do unexpected things, like learning to paraglide, or deciding to take up the saxophone. Could a computer decide to do these things just because it felt like it?

HELPFUL TOOLS

Technology can work alongside the human mind. Advanced computers can even express people's thoughts and feelings. The scientist Stephen Hawking uses a voice simulator to stand in for nerve pathways that have been damaged by disease. But even this advanced technology is obeying orders from the human being who is operating it.

In 1997, world chess champion Garry Kasparov lost to a computer. He then accused the computer of cheating!

FUZZY LOGIC

Computers follow clear instructions to give a correct answer. But they are not very good at thinking imaginatively. If someone asks you what the word "bear" means, you might think of real animals, or a cartoon bear, or a teddy bear you had as a child. A computer couldn't do this.

CONSCIOUS DECISIONS

Computers can't reproduce what goes on in your mind – that mixture of emotions, feelings, and memories that makes you unique. Your mind is aware of all of these. It's responsible for your consciousness, your way of understanding yourself and your place in the world around you. Computers can be programmed to have conversations with people. However, this is just a simulation – a pretend copy of something real. The computer is not aware of itself, and is not thinking like a person would.

DEFENSIVE ACTION

Your body is amazing! It is always on guard, ready to see off attacks by germs that could make you ill. Although you're surrounded by millions of these germs each day, your body sets up barriers to deal with most of them before they can harm you.

Even if nasty germs make it past your defensive barriers, your body has lots of weapons to do battle. Those weapons are part of your immune system. They fight to isolate and get rid of nasty invaders. Once they succeed, they remember how they won, so it will be easier to see off that type of attack next time.

Your defensive systems remain active even after they've dealt with an infection or injury. It's just as important to make sure you can heal and recover fully. Leaving that job half done would make you an easy target for more problems.

INVISIBLE ENEMIES

Most of the germs that make you unwell are either bacteria, fungi, protozoa, or viruses.

Bacteria are tiny one-celled creatures – they are everywhere around you and even inside you! Most bacteria won't hurt you, and many do useful jobs such as helping with digestion. But some bacteria are harmful and can make you ill.

Protozoa are also one-celled creatures. Most protozoa are harmless, but some cause serious diseases such as malaria and dysentery.

Fungi are tiny relatives of mushrooms that live in damp places. Athlete's foot is a fungal infection that you can catch if you don't dry your feet properly.

Viruses live inside the cells of plants or animals. Once inside a cell they take over the cell to reproduce. In humans, viruses cause illnesses such as colds, chickenpox, and flu.

GERM WARFARE

Germs are tiny, harmful living organisms. There are several different types, and they're all so small you cannot see them with the naked eye. That's why you have to be extra careful to protect yourself from them. Your body will defend itself if these germs get inside you, but you can help keep your body healthy by taking steps to stop them in their tracks.

A GOOD CLEAN

Your skin is your first line of protection against most types of infection. But it's important to keep it clean. Washing your hands thoroughly helps prevent the spread of colds, flu, food poisoning, and many other illnesses. A good tip is to sing "Happy Birthday to You" twice while you wash. Then you'll have done a good job!

WAITING TO ATTACK

You can pick up germs almost anywhere! They could be in the food you eat, on dirty door handles, or computer keyboards. Germs can even be in the air you breathe if someone has spread germs by coughing or sneezing. When you eat, germs from your hands can go in your mouth. Or rubbing your eye with a dirty finger spreads the germs in there. Luckily, your body has lots of ways of defending you from germ attack.

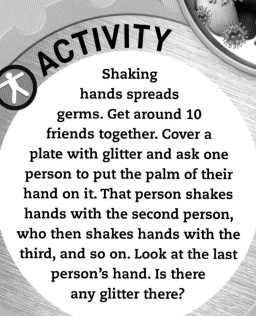

The name malaria comes from Italian words meaning "bad air", which is what people once thought caused the disease!

ACTIVITY

Shaking hands spreads germs. Get around 10 friends together. Cover a plate with glitter and ask one person to put the palm of their hand on it. That person shakes hands with the second person, who then shakes hands with the third, and so on. Look at the last person's hand. Is there any glitter there?

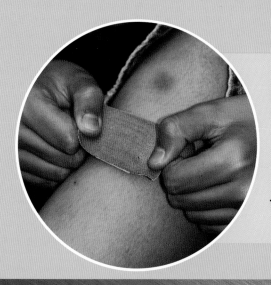

DO NOT PASS "GO"

One of the most common ways for germs to attack is through wounds, like cuts or scrapes. If your protective layer of skin is removed, then germs find it easier to enter your body. That's why it is important to dab a cut with antiseptic to clean it, and to cover it while it heals.

RAPID RESPONSE

Even with your skin protecting you, and your own good work to stay clean, germs can enter your body. That's when your immune system starts to fight back. It gets rid of some germs almost as soon as they arrive. And if germs do get past and start to make you ill, your body does its best to limit the damage.

Runny nose

Sore throat

Temperature

Aches in joints

SUFFERING THE SYMPTOMS

When you catch a cold or develop the flu, you begin to feel uncomfortable in various ways. Your nose becomes stuffed up or runny. You may have a headache or a high temperature, and your joints may begin to ache. These symptoms are usually signs that your immune system is acting to get rid of the virus. Aching joints are painful evidence of infection, but they might also be your body's way of telling you not to move around too much. That way, your body can concentrate more on fighting the infection and less on providing energy for your muscles.

MIGHTY MUCUS

Your nose is always making gooey mucus, even when you're well. Mucus stops the skin inside your nose from drying out, and it stops lots of germs from going any further into your body and making you ill. If you have a cold, your nose works even harder to fight off the infection. The mucus gets thicker and stickier. That's why you go through all of those tissues when you catch a cold!

Area where mucus is produced

AH-CHOO!

Did you know that a sneeze travels at 160 km/h (100 mph)! A sneeze is your body's way of getting rid of an irritating – or attacking – object out of your nose and mouth. Signals pass along the nerves to tell the muscles in your diaphragm, stomach, chest, and throat to work together to make that sudden blast of air. A single sneeze can get rid of 100,000 germs!

A 12-year-old girl called Donna Griffiths had a sneezing fit that lasted 978 days. It's estimated that she sneezed a million times during that period!

IT MUST BE SOMETHING I ATE!

Germs sometimes catch a ride into your body on something you eat or drink. Your body recognizes the invaders and tries to get rid of them as fast as possible. The fastest way is often vomiting or throwing up. You may feel a bit unwell after vomiting because it's such a violent act. But you will probably soon begin to feel a little better!

FIGHTING BACK

Although your body does a good job of defending itself from germ invaders – or sending them off promptly – germs do sometimes settle in for a battle. Your immune system then has to destroy these invisible invaders. It will also remember how it did the job, so that next time you'll be protected.

CODE RED!

Your blood contains cells to combat infection. Imagine that you fall and cut yourself, and the cut gets infected. On the surface, cells called platelets form a scab to stop other germs getting in. Inside, white blood cells use special chemicals to digest foreign germs. Once they've used up all of their chemicals they die, along with the attacking germs.

BLOOD, SPIT, AND TEARS

The battle for your body is fought on many different fronts, and you don't have to be cut and bleeding to risk infection. Your body can tell whether a certain type of bacteria in your mouth belongs there to help you digest – or if it's an intruder. Your saliva contains chemicals that can destroy the outer walls of invading bacteria and viruses. Your tears also contain antibodies, and can destroy germs if they get into your eyes.

SEEK AND DESTROY

Your blood contains proteins called antibodies that identify and destroy harmful germs. They are shown attacking a virus in the image on the right. Antibodies can tell the difference between dangerous germs, and the helpful bacteria that your body needs. Antibodies attach themselves to the attackers and either destroy them, or send them along to special cells that digest the attackers.

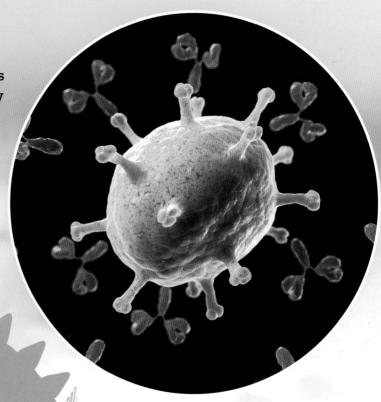

ANTIBODIES NEVER FORGET!

As it fights infection, your body uses a type of "memory" to prepare for future conflict. Once antibodies have done their job, they help other cells remember how the attackers were identified and destroyed. So the next time that type of germ attacks, your body is able to respond more quickly. That's why if you've had certain diseases, such as chickenpox or mumps, you rarely catch them again.

LYMPHATIC SYSTEM

The blood isn't the only fluid running through your body. The lymphatic system is often called your body's "drainage network". But the liquid flowing slowly through it – lymph – also contains cells that work hard to defend you against infection.

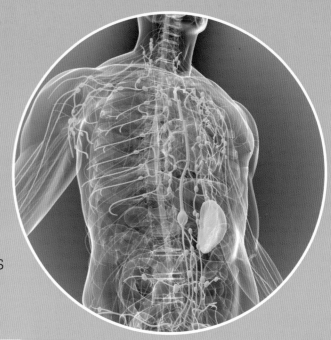

Heart

Vein

Lymph node

Lymphatic capillaries

Artery

Blood capillaries

Tissue cells

PRECIOUS TRANSPORT

The lymphatic system (shown in green on the left and above) extends across your whole body. It helps to keep your body's fluids in balance by absorbing some of the extra liquid that builds up between tissue cells and returning it to your veins. Upon entering the system, it becomes part of another liquid – lymph – which also contains wastes that need to be filtered out.

SWOLLEN GLANDS

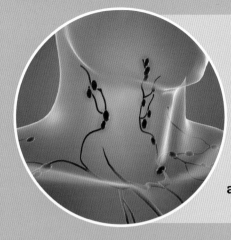

You sometimes hear a person say "I'm not well – my glands are swollen". They're probably talking about the lymph nodes (which some people call glands) on the side of their neck or under their arms. These nodes swell up when their white blood cells are battling infection. The swelling isn't an illness in itself – it's actually a sign that the body is fighting an infection.

KILLER CELLS

Different white blood cells wage war against invaders. B cells become active when an attacker has been identified. Then they produce the antibodies to fight them. T cells sometimes battle your body's own cells – if they've been altered by infection. NK (Natural Killer) cells are even more powerful than T cells.

NK cells check the protein on every cell they meet, and poison those with an unfamiliar coating!

Cervical lymph nodes (in the face and neck)

Thoracic duct (collects the lymph from around the body)

Axillary nodes (in the armpits)

FIGHTING INFECTION

The lymphatic network has another important job which connects it to your immune system. Lymph moves slowly because it's not pumped the way blood is. Your muscles squeeze it along, and it passes through small masses of tissue, called lymph nodes, along the way. These nodes contain white blood cells that identify harmful germs and destroy them. Other white blood cells produce the antibodies that scout for invaders.

Spleen (like a large lymph node – contains white blood cells that fight infection)

Cisterna chyli (lymph reservoir; filters out fat from the intestines)

Inguinal lymph nodes (in the legs and groin)

TEMPERATURE CONTROL

Your body needs to stay at a steady temperature in order to remain healthy. It's just like a car that runs poorly in the cold or overheats in hot weather. Luckily it has many ways of adjusting its temperature. It even uses that ability to keep you healthy.

HOT AND COLD

You know if you're feeling too hot or too cold. Nerves send signals to your brain to warn you. The warning is important because your body needs to stay at around 37°C (98.6°F) to work at its best. An area of your brain called the hypothalamus is very sensitive to any temperature change. It springs into action to get your body back to that ideal temperature.

WHEN IT'S COLD...

- Blood vessels near your skin's cold surface tighten, so that not much warm blood passes through them. This may make you look a bit pale!
- Tiny hairs on your skin stand up away from your skin, to try and trap some warm air around your skin.

Shivering uses energy stored in fat to power the muscles as they twitch!

SHIVER ME TIMBERS

One of the best ways your body uses to warm up is shivering. Your brain sends messages to your muscles, getting them to twitch. That twitching, or shivering, releases heat. Your jaw might even start shivering, causing your teeth to chatter.

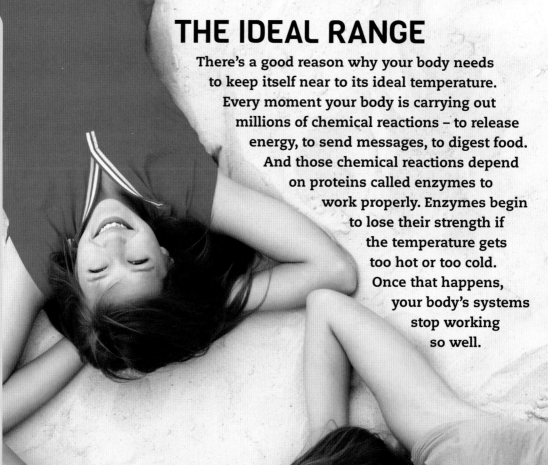

THE IDEAL RANGE

There's a good reason why your body needs to keep itself near to its ideal temperature. Every moment your body is carrying out millions of chemical reactions – to release energy, to send messages, to digest food. And those chemical reactions depend on proteins called enzymes to work properly. Enzymes begin to lose their strength if the temperature gets too hot or too cold. Once that happens, your body's systems stop working so well.

NO SWEAT!

The best way to cool down is to sweat. As sweat is mostly water, it rises or evaporates when it comes into contact with air. The water molecules go from being liquid to being a gas, and mixing with the air. They take some of their heat with them as they leave your body. You often sweat during a fever, to make sure that your body doesn't get too hot.

FEVERISH ACTIVITY

Sometimes your temperature goes up when you're fighting an infection. If it rises above 38°C (100.4°F), you probably have a fever. In your brain, the hypothalamus receives information that your body is fighting an infection. It sends out information to keep heat trapped inside, so that your temperature rises. That raised temperature, called a fever, is hot enough to help fight germs (and even destroy some of them). But it's not hot enough to damage the enzymes in your body.

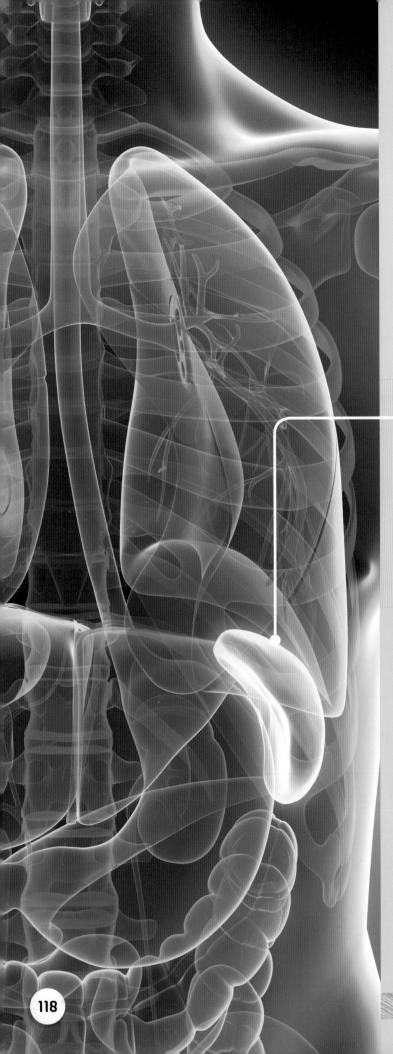

SUPER ORGANS

As well as their main jobs, many of your body's organs have other jobs to do. Your spleen, for example, is an efficient blood filter but it also teams up with the lymphatic system to do some germ-hunting. And it's not the only organ doing double – or triple – duty.

FILTER AND FIGHTER

Your spleen is an organ about the size of an adult's hand. It is tucked in the upper left of your abdomen behind your stomach. Its main job is to filter red blood cells, getting rid of those that no longer work properly and recycling the valuable iron that they contain. But your immune system also depends on the work of your spleen.

BLOOD DEFENDER

The spleen is also part of the lymphatic system. Being such an important junction for blood and lymph has real advantages. Special white blood cells called macrophages surround the dead cells that have been filtered out of the blood and carry them away. They act in the same way with germ invaders. If nasty bacteria or viruses float in, the spleen produces "defender" white bloods cell called lymphocytes. They're the cells that produce the antibodies to fight attacking germs.

TEARS: TWICE AS USEFUL

Your tears do more than just rinse your eyes out. They contain a powerful enzyme called lysozyme, which attacks invading bacteria. It eats into the outer wall of bacteria, destroying them so that they can be washed away. You also find lysozyme doing the same job in your saliva, mucus, and even in the milk that breast-feeding babies drink.

MEGA LIVER

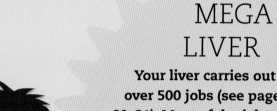

Your liver carries out over 500 jobs (see pages 80–81). Most of the jobs are to do with making and storing fuel from the food you eat, cleaning your blood, or helping you digest fats. But it also helps you recover from illness. The liver takes out the important ingredients from the medicines you take. Then, it sends them to where they're needed. It also helps to stop bleeding by causing your blood to thicken, or clot.

Bile produced by the spleen is bitter-tasting. The ancient Greeks linked the spleen to bitter, or angry, moods in people!

BRILLIANT BONES

The spongy central section of your bones, called the marrow, is a blood-cell factory. It's known mainly for producing the red blood cells that transport oxygen and nutrients throughout your body (see pages 68-69). But it also makes white blood cells and platelets that are two vital parts of your immune system.

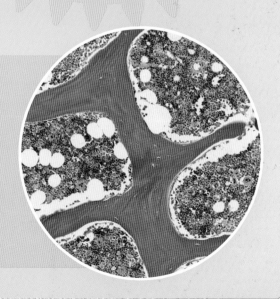

TEAMWORK

If you find yourself in a dangerous situation with a group of other people, the smart thing to do is work together. It's the same for your body's organs and systems. They all work together as a team to keep your body running smoothly. If one part isn't working as well as it should, the others come to its aid.

PARTNERS

Your immune system needs other systems to work well. One of its most important partners is the system which triggers hormones (see pages 82–83). Some of these hormones decide how sensitive your immune system is or how hard it should be working. Hormones instruct different parts of your body by delivering chemical signals. Your body's cells and tissues respond to these chemical changes. These chemical reactions produce physical changes – blood vessels might tighten or widen, muscles might begin to twitch, or more cells might be formed to scab over a cut.

Sweat glands in your feet produce around 500ml (17.5 fl oz) of sweat each day!

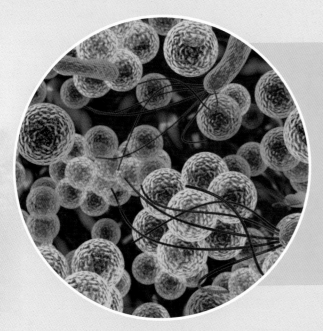

GOOD BACTERIA

Some of your body's fiercest defenders are actually bacteria. In fact, these "good bacteria" outnumber the harmful bacteria in many parts of your body. Many of them live in your intestines, ready to destroy harmful invaders. Other helpful bacteria alert the rest of your immune system about invasions.

HELPING EACH OTHER

Organs and systems team up to support each other if they are damaged or weakened. Although your spleen plays an important role in your immune system, you can survive without it – other organs and systems just have to work a little harder. Your liver takes over the filtering of your blood and your lymphatic system produces more white cells to attack invading germs.

READY TO EAT

Imagine seeing and smelling some delicious pastries. Your eyes send information about what to expect, and your nose sends signals about how good it will taste. All that information travels to your brain, which tells your mouth to water. The saliva is important for digesting the food (see pages 26–27). But your saliva also contains an enzyme that destroys harmful bacteria that may arrive with your food. So you're not just ready for a real treat – your body is guarding you against attack.

COLD SWEAT

Sweat also plays a role as part of your defensive team. It can be triggered by your nervous system. The brain recognizes a stressful situation and tells the adrenal gland to release epinephrine (see pages 82–83), which makes you sweat. Why is this? Sweat is slippery, so it might make it hard for a predator to keep hold of you. Sweat also has antibacterial properties, to help protect you from germs.

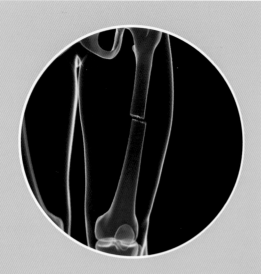

INJURY TIME

If you've ever fallen from a tree and broken your arm, sprained an ankle while running, or even had a painful paper cut, you'll know that the injury hasn't lasted forever. Your body has ways of repairing itself and helping you recover from injuries.

STICKS AND STONES...

Your bones may be strong and flexible but they can still break, especially if they are forced too hard. They're a bit like wooden pencils, or twigs, which will bend and bend until... they snap! A snap, or broken bone, is called a fracture. The first thing you'll feel if you've broken a bone is a lot of pain. It hurts so much you probably won't even try to use that arm or leg, or you risk making things even worse.

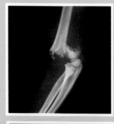

REPAIR WORK

When you break a bone, blood cells form a clot around the break. Special cells clean away floating bits of bone and kill any germs in the area. Over the next two weeks, a soft-tissue covering builds up over the fracture. Different cells, called osteoblasts, make more bone to make a hard covering. Other cells, called osteoclasts, then clear away any extra bone that has formed around the fracture. This continues until the bone is back to its original shape.

X MARKS THE SPOT

Doctors can take pictures of your bones to check whether you've had a fracture. X-rays are a type of radiation that pass through your body. The x-rays are absorbed at different rates by soft parts, like skin or muscle, and harder substances such as bones. In the x-ray picture, bones show up clearly as white shapes, just like a light shining through fog will pick out the shape of a person or car.

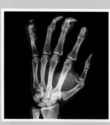
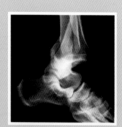
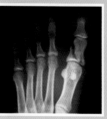
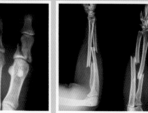
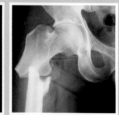

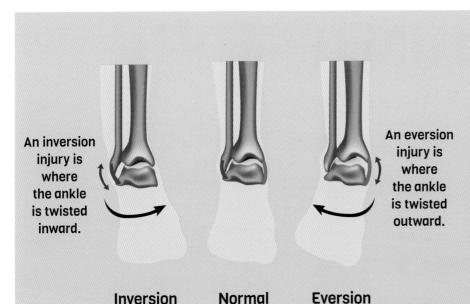

An inversion injury is where the ankle is twisted inward.

An eversion injury is where the ankle is twisted outward.

Inversion　　**Normal**　　**Eversion**

WHAT A STRAIN!

You can hurt your muscles and ligaments as well as your bones. If you stretch a muscle too much, you can strain it. Muscle strains are most common in the neck and back. If ligaments get stretched too far, the injury is called a sprain. A severe sprain is when the ligaments are torn. It's quite easy to sprain an ankle if you step on something uneven and your ankle turns suddenly.

BUMPS AND BRUISES

If you bump yourself, you may get a black or purple bruise. This forms when the injury breaks tiny blood vessels, and they leak into the tissue nearby. One of these bruises on your cheek can give you a black eye.

SOLAR BURNING

Radiation in sunlight is good for your body, but only in small doses. After that, it starts to destroy the living cells in the outer layer of your skin. This can lead to painful sunburn. Your immune system responds by opening up blood vessels to send in healing white blood cells. This increased blood flow makes your skin feel warmer and look redder. To reduce the chance of sunburn, always use sunscreen, which blocks out much of the harmful radiation from the sun.

OUTSIDE HELP

Your body is amazing at fighting disease and healing itself when it's injured. But there are times when it needs a boost to get the job done. Doctors, nurses, and other medical professionals have tools and techniques to make you better – or to stop you from getting ill in the first place. After all, prevention is better than cure.

A SHOT IN THE ARM

As a baby, you would probably have been vaccinated against a number of diseases, but you were too young to remember. Vaccination is usually a fairly painless injection. It uses your body's own antibodies to stop you catching serious diseases. A vaccination contains a mild version of that disease. It's too weak to make you feel very bad, but strong enough to get your body defending against it.

One of the best things about the way antibodies fight diseases is the "memories" they leave behind (see page 113). These are chemical records of the disease they fought, and how they got rid of it. If you're exposed to that same disease again – even in its strong version – your body can call on that information to make it harmless.

BONE PROTECTION

Although your body is able to heal a broken bone, the whole process takes time. The two bits of bone need to be lined up properly to make sure the healed bone grows back straight. Once the bone is in the right place, you'll probably have a cast put over it. That's a hard covering to keep the bone protected and stop it being bumped out of place.

A STITCH IN TIME

If you've had a deep cut, you might need stitching up. Sewing the bits of skin on either side of a cut back together stops the bleeding, helps keep out germs, and lets your body get on with healing. Most modern stitches just dissolve once they've done their job.

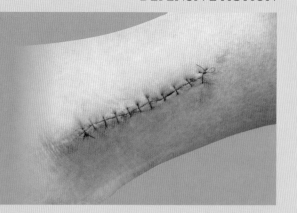

WALK OF LIFE

In the past, if people were born without limbs or lost them to injury, they would have to manage without... or use very basic, wooden replacements. Modern technology has revolutionized limb replacements, or prostheses. It has given many people the chance to type, hold a pen, stand, run, and ski. Some modern artificial limbs are even mind-controlled, so they can obey a person's thoughts.

ACTIVITY

See whether you can make an artificial hand that can pick something up. Use a pair of cooking tongs to see how effective they are. Try picking up different objects – maybe a tennis ball, a pebble, and a coin. Can you think of ways to make your "hand" work better, maybe by attaching something to it?

Over 200 years ago, cowpox, a weak cousin of the deadly disease smallpox, was used for the first vaccinations. Some people feared that patients might actually turn into cows!

GLOSSARY

amino acid An essential nutrient containing several chemical elements.

antibody A protein produced by the body to attack and destroy attackers like bacteria.

artery One of the main vessels carrying blood from the heart to other parts of the body.

atom The smallest possible particle of a chemical element.

bacteria Tiny one-celled organisms.

calorie A unit for measuring the energy contained in food.

capillary One of the smallest of the body's blood vessels.

carbohydrate A type of sugar made by plants that the body uses to produce and store energy.

cardiac Having to do with the heart.

cartilage Tough connective tissue, especially in the joints between bones.

cell The basic unit of plants and animals. Each cell has a central control, or nucleus, and is surrounded by a thin membrane.

digestion The process of breaking down food in the body to release essential nutrients.

DNA Short for Deoxyribonucleic Acid, the chemical ingredient that forms genes. Parents pass on copied parts of their DNA to their children so that some of their traits (like height and hair type) are also passed on.

eardrum A thin membrane that separates the outer ear from the middle ear. It transmits sounds from the air to the small bones of the inner ear.

element A substance that cannot be broken down into simpler substances.

energy The power to be active and perform jobs.

enzyme A special protein that helps chemical reactions occur.

fat A chemical substance that the body produces to store energy. It is stored in fat cells beneath the skin or surrounding organs.

follicle A tube-shaped cavity that contains the root of a hair.

fungi Small organisms that form part of a larger group including yeasts and mushrooms.

gene A combination of chemicals that carries information about how an organism will appear and behave.

hormone A chemical that helps to regulate processes such as reproduction and growth.

immune system The network of organs, chemicals and special cells that protects the body from disease.

ligament A band of strong tissue that connects the ends of bones or holds an organ in place.

lobe One of the divisions of the brain, which concentrates on a certain activity such as sight, memory, or emotions.

   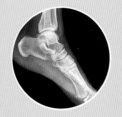

lymphatic system A network of thin tubes, like blood vessels, that transports cells to fight infection and carries a clear liquid (lymph) to take dead cells away.

marrow The soft tissue inside sections of large bone where new blood cells are produced.

membrane A thin, flexible layer of tissue around organs or cells.

metabolism The chemical processes that the body's cells use to produce energy from food, get rid of waste, and heal themselves.

mineral A chemical substance, such as iron, which is important for health but which the body cannot produce.

molecule The smallest possible unit of a substance that still behaves like that substance. A molecule is made up of two or more atoms.

neuron Also called a nerve cell, it is one of the basic cells of the nervous system.

nutrient Any substance that the body needs for energy or growth.

organ A collection of cells that work together to perform a specific function.

organelle Part of a cell that does one job.

plasma The fluid that carries the different blood cells through the body.

platelet A blood cell that helps healing by binding with other platelets when they detect a damaged blood vessel. When platelets dry, they form a scab.

protein One of the most important of all molecules in the body, protein is needed to strengthen and replace tissue in the body. Muscles and many organs are made of protein.

protozoa A tiny one-celled organism that normally lives in water or soil.

REM Rapid Eye Movement: a stage of sleep when you are most likely to have dreams.

sperm A male reproductive cell that combines with a female's egg to produce a new baby.

spinal cord A collection of nerves that runs from your brain down the middle of the back and ends at your waist. Nerves branch out from it to run to the rest of your body.

tendon A tough tissue that connects a muscle to a bone.

tissue A collection of cells that look the same and have a similar job to do in your body.

vein One of the main vessels carrying blood from different parts of the body to the heart.

virus A tiny organism that cannot grow or reproduce unless it is inside the cell of another organism.

vitamin A natural substance found in foods, but which the human body cannot produce, although it is necessary for good health.

INDEX

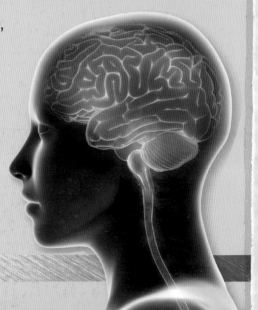